TELLING
EACH OTHER
THE TRUTH

TELLING EACH OTHER THE TRUTH

WILLIAM BACKUS

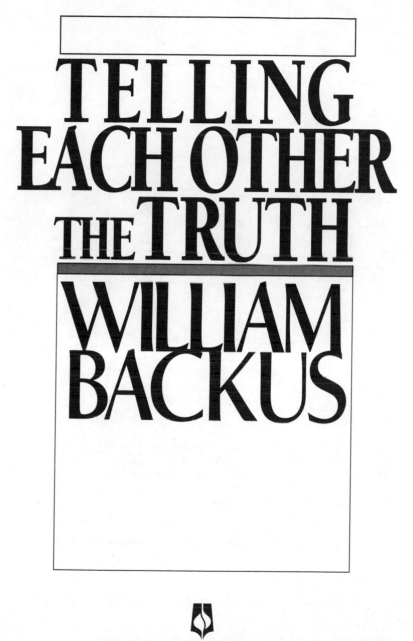

BETHANY HOUSE PUBLISHERS
Minneapolis, Minnesota 55438

Published by Bethany House Publishers
A Division of Bethany Fellowship, Inc.
6820 Auto Club Road, Minneapolis, Minnesota 55438

Printed in the United States of America

Library of Congress Cataloging in Publication Data

Backus, William D.
    Telling each other the truth.

        1. Truthfulness and falsehood.   2. Christian life—1960-
I. Title.
BJ1421.B33   1985   248.4   85-20003
ISBN 0-87123-852-7 (pbk.)

To Candy

WILLIAM BACKUS, Ph.D., is a Christian psychologist and an ordained Lutheran clergyman. He is Founder and Director of the Center for Christian Psychological Services in St. Paul, Minnesota. He and his family make their home in Forest Lake, Minnesota. He is also associate pastor of a large Lutheran church.

The Center for Christian Psychological Services receives numerous requests for referrals to licensed Christian professional counselors who use Christian cognitive therapy as set forth in Dr. Backus' books. The Center would be happy to receive from you a brief summary of your counseling experience with misbelief therapy and your qualifications, license status, and commitment to Christian truth in your practice. On the basis of such information, the Center will refer callers from your area to you. Please include a telephone number with area code, address, and the name of the facility with which you are affiliated.

The Center for Christian Psychological Services
Roseville Professional Center #435
2233 N. Hamline
St. Paul, Minnesota, 55113
(612) 633–5290

Contents

Books by Dr. Backus

Empowering Parents
   (with Candace Backus)
Finding the Freedom of Self-Control
Finding the Freedom of Self-Control Study Guide
   (with Steven Wiese)
The Good News About Worry
The Hidden Rift With God
Learning to Tell Myself the Truth
Taking Charge of Your Emotions
   (Audio tape)
Teaching Your Children to Tell Themselves the Truth
   (with Candace Backus)
Telling Each Other the Truth
Telling the Truth to Troubled People
Telling Yourself the Truth (with Marie Chapian)
Telling Yourself the Truth Study Guide
   (with Marie Chapian)
Untwisting Twisted Relationships
   (with Candace Backus)
Untwisting Twisted Relationships Study Guide
   (with Candace Backus)
What Did I Do Wrong? What Can I Do Now?
   (with Candace Backus)
Why Do I Do What I Don't Want to Do?
   (with Marie Chapian)

INTRODUCTION

"Two Hundred Lies a Day"

You don't need a book to teach you to tell the truth, right? That's what Joel thought about himself, too. He believed he was a truthful man—well, for the most part. And he certainly wouldn't have traced his current difficulties to untruthfulness. He knew he was a good doctor, too. Then why was he risking everything? Why was he putting it on the line in exchange for nothing?

He knew he was taking an enormous risk. If arrested he would be ruined. His practice would go down the drain. He might even lose his medical license. Julie would leave him—he knew that for certain. And his family would never recover from the shock and mortification.

Yet Joel continued walking toward the bar. He seemed driven. The familiar pattern of intense pressure from marital disharmony and professional responsibility seemed more than he could bear. Always at such times of stress his mind dangled before him the excitement of the forbidden—and the pressure always persisted until he gave in.

He knew what the end would be, yet he told himself that this time he would not go that far. He would only stop and watch the strippers for a few hours, have a couple of drinks, and then go home. Perhaps that would be enough. It would have to be enough. He had promised God he would clean up his act.

Home. Joel did not allow his mind to dwell on home. How shocked his patients would be if they knew what his life with

Julie had been like! Most of his patients viewed him as almost divine. What would they think if they knew he and Julie weren't talking, that they seldom got along well enough to sleep in the same bed? What would they think if they knew of the feelings (Were they angry feelings?) he had locked inside himself?

How would Julie react if she knew? He failed to notice a quick thrill of satisfaction at the thought of Julie discovering his secret. It would hurt her, and she deserved to be hurt. But he would never tell. She mustn't find out. Still, he knew dimly that in some curious way he was getting even, taunting her, punishing her, rubbing her nose in her coldness, acting out his anger at her this very moment.

She would never know. She *must* not find out. For he knew the course he was on would not stop with a couple of drinks and a show. It would end as it had always ended. He would find a prostitute and go home with her. It was his act of "communication" directed at the Julie he carried in his mind. The real Julie must not know.

Here was communication gone so awry that it never communicated at all! Julie would also never know that he was angry. He wouldn't tell her. He didn't know how. And if he did tell her, she wouldn't know how to answer. So instead of telling each other the truth, this couple had learned to "stuff it." And the result was Joel's gross, sinful, pathological, guilt-ridden misbehavior. Joel, like most people, did not think he needed to learn how to tell Julie the truth about himself and the needs and feelings he harbored.

Most people who are likely to read this book were taught long ago not to lie. The lesson usually comes early in life. The first time a child makes up a story to avoid parental wrath, he may discover that the penalty for his inventive genius is worse than if he had truthfully admitted his trespass.

If you are fortunate enough to have been reared by parents whose compassion, love, and respect for morality were consistent, you will have acquired the truth habit to the point where you wouldn't dream of lying—in most situations. You will hardly believe you need a book to teach you to speak the truth.

Nonetheless, most people, even most moral people—like us—slip around the truth without even realizing it. Yes, we have learned the difference between truth and lies. But to an extent we don't fully realize, the culture desensitizes us to falsehood, immunizes us to its evils, simmers us in a broth of untruth, and numbs us to the uncounted lies we hear each day. So we eventually take certain untruths for granted and hear them without amazement or shock.

Someone calculated that each of us tells 200 lies each day! Yet we believe ourselves to be honest, truthful folk. In fact, we'd swear to it—and chances are, we'd be swearing to an untruth. It's so much easier to "call in sick" than to go to work when relatives we like are visiting. Few people think twice before insisting to the arresting officer that they were not driving as fast as he claims they were. Most errors on tax returns occur in favor of the taxpayer, attesting to our habit of nudging reality in our own direction. The marriage counselor who interviews each partner separately can hardly believe he is hearing about the same relationship—the two versions vary so sharply.

The consequences of this built-in disregard for truth dog our tracks. Most of the time we barely notice how they underscore human faithlessness. Banks can't cash checks for strangers; stores won't take merchandise returned without a sales slip; TV monitors scan the aisles to catch furtive hands; ushers on guard make sure we don't see two movies for the price of one; in the days when virtue was important, young women learned to be wary of young men with a "line"; all America knows what a dead bolt lock is; insurance against the dishonesty of others costs us hard-earned resources; dogs, alarm systems, fences, walls, vaults, lockers, safe-deposit boxes, false bottoms, secret pockets, chains, combinations, bars, bolts, padlocks, polygraphs, voice analyzers, bloodhounds—all provide some of the most obvious signs of everyday falsehood.

LIES AND HUMAN MISERY

But the less obvious markers of lies at work need attention. Untruths devastate our plans, corrupt our characters, disrupt our relationships, shred our spirits, and putrify our sweetest daydreams.

We become insensitive to the lies because our daily life has inured us to noise. It comes pouring at us from a hundred loud-speakers during nearly every waking moment. What we hear is often false; worse, we take falsehood for granted.

Falsehoods are sung, shouted and whispered to us. False-hoods hypnotize and cajole us to buy soap, magazines, tomb-stones, dish detergent, condominiums, books, fly spray, laxa-tives, scuba lessons, medical care, beer, vacation cruises, and dating services. But even more insidious, we are sold false *ideas*; we are told what to think, and are thus seduced into believing false notions about who we are, what we must have, where we really came from, what life is all about, and how we ought to live. Much that is offered on the idea market consists of lies.

Here is how those lies affect us: Perhaps we are not happy. Ask most of us why we are miserable and we will tell you that the problem lies outside ourselves; or if it lies within ourselves we will blame it on the lack of something within, some attribute which leads to happiness. "God," we whine, "why don't you just give me that one thing I lack. Then I'll be happy." We imagine our misery exists because God won't loosen up and give a little. It would be so easy for Him! Why doesn't He?

This is perhaps the biggest lie of all. The notion that the cause of our unhappiness lies elsewhere creates precisely that state of hopelessness the enemy so fervently desires: The "I can't and God won't" situation of utter despair.

Even the secular psychologist who keeps up with his reading knows better. Cognitive psychology, pioneered by Ellis, Beck, Mahoney, Meichenbaum, Novaco, and many other researchers, certainly knows better. For more than a decade, these psychol-ogists have found wanting the old Skinnerian behaviorism which insisted man is no different from the laboratory animal insofar as the mechanisms governing his behavior are concerned. If the laboratory rat could be taught to press a lever by rewarding him with pellets of pressed barley, then psychologists could teach man to save his soul by rewarding him for correct responses. The social learning and cognitive behavioral psychologists did not exactly repudiate Skinner's principles, they merely added something. Yet the addition was crucial. They discovered that, unlike the laboratory rat, man *thinks*. He assesses, appraises, and evaluates, supplying meaning to events.

It is the content of human thinking that makes the difference between misery and happiness. What matters is not the event, but how a person appraises and evaluates the event. What occurs outside him does not make him joyful or wretched, angry or benevolent, peaceful or turbulent. What he *believes* about the event makes all the difference.

So, by a quirk in the development of psychological thought, theoreticians and clinicians have come strikingly close to saying what the Scriptures say: "As he thinketh in his heart, so is he" (Prov. 23:7), and, "According to your faith, so be it unto you" (Matt. 9:29). Psychologists now acknowledge that faith saves. But most Christians have failed to note the revolutionary implications of these biblical teachings. Therefore, as is so often the case, God had to send messengers from the secular world to open our eyes to the treasure we have.

Here's the good news: If you will learn to tell yourself the truth, learn to believe it "up front," where you live, rather than stow it in some mental file labeled "pure doctrine" (to be pulled out when you need to argue with someone), you can control your own happiness and defeat every wile of the enemy. That is why Jesus said, "The truth shall make you free" (John 8:32).

WHAT IS TRUTH?

Pontius Pilate, quoted frequently on the subject, did not know what truth is. Furthermore, he thought no one else knew either. Perhaps he was ahead of his time. One reason for the truth deficit in today's secular culture is the loss of the logical and philosophical underpinnings for truth once furnished by the Christian faith. The result is relativism. Francis Schaeffer devoted a lifetime of effort to tracing the results of this loss and advancing a powerful remedy.

Relativism, the naive notion that anybody's truth is as good as anybody else's, has gained a firm foothold among psychologists, though no psychologist could conceivably live or work in faithful adherence to it. Many studies have demonstrated that even the psychotherapist who thinks he does value-neutral therapy actually imposes his values on his patient. Such value-setting does not square well with the relativistic notion that each person's truth is just fine for his own needs. After all, if the relativistic psychologist acts in harmony with his professed philosophy, he will not push his own values or his own truth. He will recognize the patient's truth and values as equal with his.

Scientific studies suggest that it's a good thing relativistic psychologists aren't consistent enough to practice their relativism, for if they did their patients wouldn't get better. Improvement seems to be associated with change in the patient's values—in the direction of the therapist's values.

In contrast to contemporary relativism, this book advances the view that truth is objective (what Schaeffer calls "true truth" to distinguish it from relativistic "truth"). Beliefs corresponding with reality are objectively true, while beliefs at variance with reality are objectively false. Truth is what corresponds to the way things are. Falsehood is what does not correspond to objective reality.

THE STARTING POINT IS GOD

God is truth, according to Scripture. He is the final reality, the ultimate ground of all other reality. As the theologian-philosopher might put it, God is a non-contingent Being, meaning He doesn't owe His reality to anything else—so that if everything else were to disappear from existence, God would still exist.

When the Bible speaks of God as true, or as "the Truth," its writers have a different meaning in mind from that of the philosophers. Hebrew thought contains no static concepts. "God is true" for Bible authors means "God comes true." They are claiming that God always brings what He says to pass. The things God says must happen. "Let there be light" spoken by God creates a reality called "light." God's promises given through the prophets must come true in the Baby finally born in a barn. What God *says* is bound to *be*. Thus it is that God is "the Truth."

"I am the . . . Truth," Jesus said of himself in one of the most breathtaking claims ever made by a non-psychotic human being. He did not mean merely that He always *told* the truth, although He certainly spoke more truth in His three years of ministry than anyone who has ever set foot on the planet. What Jesus meant, as shown by careful study of the Gospel of John, is that He is *God coming true*. He is the concrete reality God promised through all the prophets. In Him the God who is Truth comes true. Every one of God's promises takes on concrete reality in the person of Jesus. When we look at Him we are looking at God's Word made concrete reality. So Jesus is "the Truth."

Even as God himself is Truth, as Jesus is the Truth of God come true, God's Word—what God says—*must*, absolutely must, be true and come to pass. His Word never asserts anything contrary to reality because reality must line up with whatever God's Word says.

Although God has spoken often to us, the essence of God's message to man is found in the Judeo-Christian Scriptures. These books are the very words given by God through inspired writers. Therefore what they tell us must be so. They are truth in the sense that they cannot possibly tell us anything contrary to final reality. What they say must either be reality already or must come to pass in the future.

If the biblical record is absolute truth, the Bible is utterly reliable. With it, according to Paul in 2 Timothy 3:16, 17, we can profitably use the Bible to correct our wrong notions about reality. With the Bible as a guide, we can learn to tell ourselves the truth about ultimate reality, truth we could not know in any other way.

TRUTH THROUGH REASON AND THE EVIDENCE OF OUR SENSES

According to the Bible, the God who made the universe also constructed our eyes, ears and other senses. He invented our reasoning brain, too. He designed all these tools specifically to fit His created reality. In other words, He who made the universe also made our reason and our senses to convey truth about the universe to our minds. That is why we can trust observation, experiment, mathematics, and science as guides to truth.

The truth we are discussing includes the sort of everyday truth that is exemplified by the statement, "I am now reading a book." It includes the sort of everyday truth which reports, reliably, to another person, "What you just said hurt my feelings," or, "I love you," or, "It's snowing outside."

One important note: This empirical and rational truth must remain subject to correction by God's revealed Word. This kind of truth gains its validity by God's revelation and therefore cannot sit in judgment on that revelation. When man tries to use his senses and reasoning to judge God's Word, he becomes hopelessly lost in a quagmire of misbelief—a quagmire in which some contemporary theology is stuck. A fascinating book on this subject, *The Suicide of Christian Theology* by John Warwick Montgomery (Bethany House Publishers, 1970), may help you understand in what way theology which enthrones reason has lost the truth.

FIRST, TELL YOURSELF THE TRUTH

Some readers will not yet have come to terms with the untruths they are daily communicating to themselves. God desires "truth in the inward parts" (i.e., He wants you to learn to speak truth to yourself). Moreover, you can become contented and happy only by tasting the freedom truth can bring to your innermost parts. You can discover more about speaking truth to yourself by studying two other books: *Telling Yourself the Truth* and *Why Do I Do What I Don't Want To Do?*—both by Marie Chapian and me (published by Bethany House Publishers).

THE POWER OF TRUTH BETWEEN PEOPLE

This book, also about the power and effectiveness of truth, demonstrates the application of truth in *relationships*. Just as the truth, properly believed and used, has power to create emotional health within the individual, truth can also heal relationships. Truth heals what hurts *between* people as well as what hurts *inside* them.

See how our customs of speech frequently skirt the truth! We say, "I'd love to have you come," when we don't want the other person to come at all. We say, "Your wishes are all that matter to me," and then get angry when the other person tells us honestly what he wants. We hide what we really want and then act cross when others fail to discern our heart's desires. We fear honest refusals, so we agree to things we dislike. We explain to others why we simply *must* do something when the truth is we *want* to do it—and there is no *must* to it. We manipulate others with expressions intended to arouse guilt before God, when our real motive is to control their behavior.

Is it any wonder our relationships often hang by a thread? Or that our attempts at communication don't work? Is it any wonder nobody really knows us? Or that we can't be as close to other human beings as we can to our dogs and cats? The truth can set relationships free, as it can set the individual free. This book is an instruction manual to help us make a beginning. From it we can learn to embed the truth in our everyday utterances. Not harsh truth, but truth spoken in love.

LIVING RESULTS OF TRUTH BETWEEN PEOPLE[1]

I have seen truth heal living relationships between living people. Sometimes I have an opportunity to introduce one party in a troubled relationship to the art of telling the truth in love. Before long, reports of improvement trickle in: "She has noticed the change in the way I behave, and she likes it! What's really amazing is that she's changing too." "I think my husband may want to come in. I told him I had been seeing you and he didn't hit the ceiling. He thought something had happened to make me different. Well, Doctor, I'll tell you something: he's changed too. He doesn't stay in his silent moods for days at a time anymore. And it's been weeks since he lost his temper and swore at me."

At first, these reports astonished me. I chalked them up to coincidence. Why? Because it is a truism in the therapy business that the therapist must have both people in front of him to effect change in a relationship. Marriages are not supposed

---

[1]A very important note about cases cited in this book: Every psychotherapist could create a fascinating book by merely publishing his case records. However, he owes his clients strict confidentiality. Conversations in the consulting room are privileged, and must not be revealed to anyone. For this reason, although the case materials in these are true-to-life, they are composites rather than specific cases. Identifying features have been changed, details have been merged, histories have been blended, with the result that all are beyond recognition.

to be helped much when the therapist works with only one partner.

I therefore always stipulate at the outset that our target for change will be the behavior of the patient. I deliberately avoid shooting for major changes in the behavior of someone who is not present in the sessions. Instead, I concentrate on the patient, aim at altering the patient's behavior by substituting truth-in-love in place of the old, misbelief-based behavior. The patient and I agree at the outset to consider our work successful if he changes in ways which satisfy him. We will never gauge improvement on the basis of whether or not the absent partner changes, but only on positive improvement in the patient.

But experience has proven otherwise. In spite of this careful focus on the patient, reports of change in the absent partner keep coming in. In case after case, not only does my patient report that he is doing better and feeling better, but also that the behavior of the *other* person in the troubled relationship has improved!

The principles taught in this book can improve relationships. I urge you, however, as I urge my clients, to aim strictly at improving your own speech and actions, recognizing that the other person's behavior is his own responsibility, and changing it is God's business. This ends the effort to control that person, and thus relieves you of a great burden. If you focus on bringing your own words and deeds into line with loving truth, you will be gratified with success, whether or not your spouse or friend shapes up according to your wishes.

THE IMPORTANCE OF EFFORT

Reading a book is, for some people, a struggle. They are apt to think, therefore, that reading alone will generate osmotic pressure sufficient to soak change into their tissues. Not so.

This attitude resembles what many people think when they visit a professional counselor. They arrive at their first clinical appointment believing their own effort ends at that point. "Now the doctor will fix me up," they tell themselves as they relax into the deep recliner (which most of my clients choose). Not so. One of the first things a client must learn if he is to get well is that change comes hard. He must work at it. If he doesn't want to work, he will have to anyhow, since I don't know how to help anyone who won't work.

You will often read instructions in this book for changing something. Plan to work hard at following those instructions. Make the effort to keep logs, teach yourself new responses, seek out opportunities, and put the instructions into practice. If you merely read, not much will change. If you read and *work*, putting your new information into practice, you will change the bad habits of a lifetime and success will be yours.

Your goal may seem too modest. Perhaps changing someone else would seem a much more worthy accomplishment to you. It won't work. Focus rather on changing the one person in the world whose behavior you can control: *yourself.*

Work with this book to develop the habit of truthful speech in all your relationships. The payoff for this will be the satisfaction of seeing the change in your dialogue with others. If others change, too, so much the better. And, in my experience, contrary to what I was taught to expect, others do change at times. But even if they don't, *you* can. And there is great satisfaction in knowing that you are acting as God would want you to act.

That is the goal: Conforming to the clear life standard of God's Word. May the Spirit of Truth take you by the hand and guide you over each exciting step on the path toward truthful, loving speech.

William Backus
Forest Lake, Minnesota
Christmas, 1984

CHAPTER ONE

Say What You Want to Say

"You wanna know what I shoulda told him?"

Pauline's face was livid, her fury obvious. She then recited the speech she wished she'd made to the garage foreman. She was sure he had cheated her. But she made the speech to her friend, Jody.

To the foreman she'd muttered only, "Are you sure this is right?" He said he was. She thought otherwise, but she only clamped her lips together as she silently wrote out her check for the repair bill. Her rage infused her acting with real conviction—but it was only acting. Furthermore, if she had told the foreman what she "shoulda," it would have been an angry blast pushing him to retaliate in kind.

But if she had given it more thought, Pauline would have concluded what most of us have decided in our sober moments: Better to speak simple, straightforward truth than to stuff your feelings and say nothing or to let your anger fly.

WHAT'S THE SECRET?

What makes a relationship between people good? A heart hungry for closeness to other human beings? Is it enough just to want closeness?

Is the secret hidden in something mysterious called "personality"? Or can you make a lot of close friends if you just read a great deal, have more information than the *Encyclopedia Britannica*, and spout it off at every opportunity?

Do you try to make it by being smarter than everyone else and showing people how well you've succeeded? Do you try to get along better with people by stuffing your anger and always being Mr. Nice Guy? So why do you sometimes feel as though you can't get along with *anybody*?

Does it seem that the more you give in and go along, the harder it is to have solid, positive relationships? Do you find that your explosions only blow right back in your face? Has the whole business of relationships seemed such a mystery you've thrown in the sponge and given up?

How do you break into a group and become a part of it? How do you talk to someone you've never met before when all you want to do is socialize? How do you ask others for what you want? Should you forget it, keep quiet, and hope they'll guess? When others are doing what you don't want them to do, are you stymied because you don't know how to tell them what you feel?

The secret is *truth talk*—telling each other the truth, as the title of this book suggests. And we will pay attention to an important qualification: The truth must be told in love.

TRUTH TALK

Truth talk is what this book is all about. If you will work through these pages with the aim of learning the skills of truth talk, you will earn rich dividends on your investment. You will experience closeness and new freedom in your relationships. One person alone can improve many relationships by mastering the skills and the spiritual depth of truth talk. If two people practice truth talk together, their relationship will achieve remarkable unity. Such relationships reward rather than punish, release rather than bind, and relax rather than stress. Most people have to acquire the skills of truth talk late in life, since these skills usually have not been taught to children. But once learned, truth talk proves its worth.

To get yourself off to a good start, study the fourth chapter of Ephesians. There you will discover the principle underlying this book. Truth spoken in love keeps interactions between people smooth and rewarding. In this chapter Paul describes the Body of Christ. He says Christians, members of that body, are connected to one another by joints. If those joints are arthritic so that contacts between members are abrasive and poorly lubricated, the body itself will creak and falter. When the joints are working smoothly, the body's movements will be effective and efficient. In this brilliant chapter, Paul shows that telling each other the truth is what makes the members relate smoothly. He calls it "speaking the truth in love." Truth is the oil which lubricates the joints in the Body of Christ.

Paul wants his readers to understand the vital importance of truthful and loving speech:

> Therefore, putting away falsehood, let every one speak the truth with his neighbor, for we are members one of another. Be angry but do not sin; do not let the sun go down on your anger, and give no opportunity to the devil. . . . Let no evil talk come out of your mouths, but only such as is good for edifying, as fits the occasion, that it may impart grace to those who hear. . . . Let all bitterness and wrath and anger and clamor and slander be put away from you with all malice, and be kind to one another, tenderhearted, forgiving one another, as God in Christ forgave you. (Eph. 4:25–32, RSV)

CARRIE AND ROGER

When I first saw Carrie, she complained, "My husband and I have nothing between us but trouble." I asked Roger to come in with her, and we three took a good look at some of the patterns in their talk with one another. Their relationship could have been aptly described as a creaky, arthritic joint in the Body of Christ.

Experience has taught me that a relationship in trouble is a relationship in which people aren't telling each other the truth. And what they are telling each other is often not said in love. Thus, the joint between them, unlubricated, grinds and squeaks, and may even bring the relationship to a painful halt. In any kind of relationship, people are often guarded and protective about themselves, fearful of revealing their inner reality to others. Instead of revealing the truth inside their hearts, they stick to safe platitudes about weather and politics. Some people seldom reveal anything of themselves, even after considerable familiarity in a relationship. These same folks rarely guess the reason for the inevitable consequences: When others don't show much liking for them, it is often because others have been given very little to like, very little to know.

In cases such as that of Carrie and Roger, people frequently think they've been telling each other unvarnished truth. As this troubled couple discovered, however, they have not been doing so. They've just been throwing unvarnished barbs. Inhibitions, misdirected training, and unrealistic guilt keep them from saying simply and truthfully what they want, like, don't want, and don't like. They find it hard to admit they are hurt or angry, or to ask one another directly to change something. It's beyond them to give a positive word or to receive a word of correction—or even to receive a compliment!

After a few sessions it became clear that Carrie and Roger had developed patterns of speech which substituted indirect statements for straightforward truth. This damaged their feelings and wounded their relationship. When, together, we observed closely the way they dealt with disagreements, we saw that, instead of simple truth, they used devices such as these:

1. Their dealings with each other were nearly always indirect. They seldom "came right out and said" what they meant.
2. They often used questions rather than statements when statements would have been more truthful—because they were not really seeking information, but rather trying to impart it. Example: "Wouldn't you like to get some counseling for our problems?" is the way Carrie asked Roger to attend counseling sessions with her.
3. They both said "you" when they meant "I." "Do *you* want to go to the movies?" meant, in both of their mouths, "*I* want to go to the movies."
4. They both tried to change each other's plans or actions by generating guilt. Example: "You never ask me what I'd like for dinner and then you expect me to be grateful to you for fixing it!" or, "Can't you, once in a while, consider my feelings?"
5. They regularly resorted to put-downs and labels. Example: "You are just thoughtless—that's all there is to it."
6. They often used language (inappropriately) implying obli-

gation and even moral necessity rather than simple requests. Example: "You should . . ." or, "You ought to . . ." rather than the simple, "I want you to . . ." which would have been true.

7. They almost never expressed heartfelt positive feelings toward one another, seldom gave each other compliments, and rarely expressed appreciation and gratitude. They never thought of going out of their way to perform acts of love for one another.

8. Sometimes they didn't talk at all and communicated only with actions. Carrie would slam doors or bang things around as she worked. Roger would fall silent. The old saying that actions speak louder than words may be so, but they don't speak as accurately!

People routinely substitute these devices for truthful communication in troubled relationships, especially in stressed marriages or between roommates and friends. Some people have never communicated truthfully with their parents or their children. Even so, most people seem to believe firmly they already tell each other the truth. Few realize the extent to which the meanings of their words are left to be guessed at and to which their desires are veiled behind indirection and ambiguity. They live without integrity.

INTEGRITY

In a relationship without integrity, people leave each other to guess what the truth is. They play games with each other, then they rationalize these games by telling themselves, "If he loved me, he would be sensitive to my needs and I wouldn't have to tell him what they are."

If you have a relationship you would like to test for integrity, try a device I sometimes employ in the clinic. You and the other person first list the things you most want from each other. Then make a second list of your guesses as to what the other's list contains. Quite often the lists will be surprisingly different. If they are, the point I am making will be driven home: People don't tell each other their true wants and needs.

Roger, for instance, thought Carrie wanted him to make more money and get a promotion. These things didn't appear anywhere on Carrie's list of her desires. Carrie thought Roger would say he wanted her to leave him alone. Instead, Roger revealed his deep desire for Carrie's companionship and closeness.

Most of us know more about ourselves than we allow anyone else to discover. A few succeed in hiding nearly everything from others. According to international law, prisoners of war are required to give only name, rank, and serial number when they are captured. That's about all some of us allow others to know about us. We have had a breakdown of integrity.

Integrity is a word seldom encountered these days, except perhaps among politicians trying to persuade you to vote for them. But it is a big word in the Bible. We need to recover what integrity stands for: "A righteous man who walks in his integrity—blessed are his sons after him!" (Prov. 20:7, RSV).

The word integrity occurs, among other places, in Psalm 7:8: ". . . judge me, O LORD . . . according to the integrity that is in me." There and elsewhere in the Bible, it stands for manifesting in life and words the truth a person knows and possesses in his heart. When he knows the truth about what he is within and then allows that truth to surface, he has integrity.

The word integrity comes from the Latin *integer*, meaning a whole number, not a fraction. The concept behind personal integrity is wholeness. When a person is the same without as within, when what others know about him is the same truth he knows about himself, he has integrity.

When someone knows the truth about himself and tries to hide it from others, he lacks integrity. The person hiding what he really is becomes a fraction, not a whole number. Some people make a habit of hiding themselves from others. They, like prisoners of war, give only what they must give—no more than name, rank, and serial number.

I sometimes discover the level of a person's integrity by administering a psychological test. The MMPI (Minnesota Multiphasic Personality Inventory), my favorite clinical psychological test, has several validity scales designed to reveal to the psychologist when a person taking the test is trying to hide what he truly knows himself to be. A high score on some of these scales may point to lack of integrity. When I interview a client who has scored high on the validity scales, I can witness for myself his reluctance to reveal much of anything about himself. Instead of telling me of his own pain and misery, he will concentrate on describing how others cause him grief and trouble.

Carrie and Roger had the same difficulty with each other. Their interpersonal troubles were caused by things they believed which were actually untrue. These beliefs were destroying their integrity and their marriage.

They had both been raised in similar environments. They had been taught that it is critically important to look good. Their parents had told them repeatedly, "You must always appear before others with your best foot forward," and, "Watch your public image, it's your most important possession." Carrie and Roger had even been told that their Christian witness would be ineffective unless they always appeared positive, happy, and perfectly righteous—even when they felt just the opposite inside.

Their learned, habitual social behaviors robbed them of integrity and turned them into straw people, hollow shells whose dealings with others amounted to "faking it" much of the time. Nobody knew them and they did not know each other. They were duped by a grand *misbelief*:[1]

"I must always appear perfect on the outside, even when I am very different on the inside."

I had to work hard to convince Roger and Carrie that learning the truth about themselves and revealing that truth to others was not contrary to God's will, for they had long believed

---

[1]Misbelief: A belief which is contrary to Christian truth or everyday fact, planted in our minds by the devil, nurtured by our sinful old man, and repeated over and over to ourselves. Misbeliefs lead to neurosis, bad behavior, and misery. Readers unacquainted with the term should consult *Telling Yourself the Truth* by Marie Chapian and William Backus, published by Bethany House Publishers.

that God wanted them to put up a front—they called it "giving a positive witness." This is exactly what God *doesn't* want. Paul wrote that life among Christians should be marked by speaking the truth, not by speaking pleasantries that others may want to hear. He certainly didn't mean that the merely innocuous is all that should come out of our mouths.

"BEING A GOOD SPORT" VS. TELLING THE TRUTH

Roger had been making little "humorous" remarks about Carrie; remarks which hurt. She, however, wanted to appear as a person who "can take a joke" so she didn't tell her husband how unfunny his wisecracks appeared to her. When Carrie broached the subject in their next counseling session, Roger seemed surprised. "I was just trying to have a little fun with you," he explained lamely. As we talked together, however, Roger began to reveal that anger at Carrie lay festering under the surface and had been bubbling up in his "humorous" cracks.

When Roger's resentment was finally exposed, everything made sense. It seems Carrie had been reading a novel that afternoon, while Roger raced against the clock to finish the long list of household chores he had been saving for Saturday. And though it was irritating to be so much busier than Carrie, he tried to be a "good sport" about it all, squelch his anger, and say nothing. For her part, Carrie squelched her negative feelings about his hostile wisecracks. Both had been trying to look perfect, calm, and serene when inside they were hurt and angry. Another misbelief:

> **"It is more important to look good than to speak the truth in love."**

By learning to tell one another the truth, to own up honestly to their negative feelings, they became able—with little or no misery—to resolve such situations. By being willing to show one another something besides pleasantries, they began to avoid long range unpleasantness. Carrie and Roger had to work hard to acquire the new habits of integrity set forth in this book. But as they began to tell each other the truth about themselves, they also began to discover a real relationship growing out of their increasing integrity. And they began to prize and appreciate the power of the truth to deepen love and create closeness.

You can also use the material presented in this book to discover your communication habits, and to determine when and where they depart from the scriptural norm of truth-telling. If you work on changing those miscommunication habits, you can improve your relationships with others in marriage, friendships, and everyday interactions with other human beings— especially fellow Christians. Members of the Body of Christ can actually experience closeness and oneness if they will allow the Spirit of Truth to work truth into their lives and conversations.

Do you sometimes put other considerations ahead of telling others the truth? Below is a checklist of common misbeliefs used by people veiling, hiding, or distorting the truth. You might find some of your own self-talk sentences among them.

CHECKLIST OF REASONS FOR HIDING THE TRUTH

_____ I can't tell Myrtle I don't want to go to the movies with her. It might hurt her feelings.

_____ I can't tell John his interrupting bothers me. He might get offended.

_____ I'll tell Mother we have other plans. We don't, but we can't tell her the truth: we're just too tired to have her visit right now. That would upset her because she wouldn't think the reason is good enough.

_____ I can't tell them I'm a Christian. They'd think that's weird!

_____ I can't tell them I'm busy praying and can't talk to them now. They'd think I'm trying to be super-spiritual or something.

_____ I don't want to date Harold, so I'll tell him I'm going to be out of town. Then I won't make him feel so bad.

_____ I can't tell Nick I put off answering his letter, so I need to make up some reasons for my delay.

_____ I'll say I feel fine because Christians aren't supposed to be as depressed as I am right now.

_____ I can't admit that I'm angry because Christians are always supposed to be in control.

_____ I can't tell Ed I don't like his talking to others about me because he'll come up with something he doesn't like about me—and I can't stand that.

_____ I can't say what I really think to my wife because we'd get into a fight and I want peace at home.

This list, of course, is not exhaustive. You may be able to add other examples of the kind of rationalizing misbelief that truth-veilers use to support their not speaking truth in love.

FOR REVIEW, PRAYER AND DISCUSSION

1. Study Psalm 5 carefully. Note the references to those who speak lies, are deceitful, and have no truth in their mouths. Note how they flatter with their tongues, and pay attention to what is said about the relationship between such people and the Lord.
2. How can learning to tell others the truth result in new freedom in relationships for you?
3. Do you think the skills of truth talk typically have been taught to children? Why do you think this? Do you think these skills should be taught to children?
4. What, according to Ephesians 4, is the place of truth in the Body of Christ?
5. What was the basic cause of the trouble between Carrie and Roger?
6. What are some kinds of things that are hard for people like Carrie and Roger to say?
7. What does "Wouldn't you like to. . .?" really mean in the mouths of Carrie and Roger?
8. Give an example of a person saying "you" when he means "I."
9. Devise a typical guilt-generating statement which might be used by a husband or wife.
10. Explain what integrity is.
11. Give a misbelief which mars integrity.

CHAPTER TWO

Nothing's Wrong with Saying "I"

Sometime during my formative years I learned that the pronoun "I" should be avoided. I should talk about others, not about myself. And if discourse about myself can't be avoided, I should use circumlocutions instead of the personal pronoun, first person singular, nominative case.

It is especially important, insisted one of my mentors of long ago, to avoid saying "I" in written material such as letters. So I resorted to expressions such as, "The movie, *Thin Ice*, was attended last Saturday afternoon with friends. Bikes were ridden to the theater. It was all much enjoyed." I was careful to write that way, instead of saying, "Last Saturday I went to a movie with my friends. I rode my bike and enjoyed the picture a lot." Somehow people consider it egotistical, vain, self-centered and unchristian to use the pronoun created especially to stand, in the subject of an English sentence, in place of the speaker's name.

Others must have been taught similarly. I have found my clergy friends frequently avoiding "I" by saying "we" instead: "We love you all very much and we are delighted to be back in the pulpit today," or, "We had a fine holiday, but we are glad to be back at our desk again, serving in your midst." What are they trying to do? Use the plural of majesty? I don't think so. It's simply that they have the creepy feeling that using "I" would bring the rejection and judgment of others. They were probably taught that the pronoun "I" is a no-no. This is a misbelief if I ever heard one.

This studied avoidance of a perfectly good word, for which there is no satisfactory substitute, seems to me to be silly. Frequently, however, this habit is knit together with a number of similar devices which serve to conceal the truth in our communication. We might call them devices for miscommunication. They arise out of misbeliefs, sincerely held, no doubt, from childhood; but wrong, nonetheless.

SINCERELY WRONG MISBELIEVING

I have found through hours of conversation with others, much of it dealing with problems which arise from miscommunication, that most people sincerely believe the following untrue notions:

- I must not say what I feel unless it is positive and pleasing to others.
- I must never say "I'm hurt."
- I must never say "I'm angry."
- I must never say "I'm full of doubt."
- I must never say "I don't trust you."
- I must never reveal my sense of inadequacy. Rather, I should hide it from others at all costs.
- If others knew my innermost feelings, they might dislike or reject me, or even punish me in some way for having feelings they don't like or respect.
- I'm the only one who has feelings like these.
- I must not use the word "I" because using that word is self-centered and wrong.
- Revealing myself is self-centered and wrong since people should never talk about themselves.

A CASE OF CHURCH PHOBIA

"Thump-bumpety-bump-bump-bump" went Carla's heart. The accelerated pounding frightened her. And it happened every time she went to church these days. She would sit down hopefully, trying her best to believe that today would be the day she'd be rid of her anxious feelings. But before long, the tension would steal over her, and all the discomfort and fear would return.

Carla felt like walking out. She was afraid of the feelings which came over her when she sat still. But Carla was even more afraid of leaving in the middle of the service. She was terrified that someone else might notice and guess that she was hurting inside. So the tension and anxiety would increase until Carla began to believe she would surely pass out or perhaps even drop dead.

I suggested that she could easily get up and walk out of the service if she chose, then return when she felt better.

"Oh, dear! I couldn't do that! Why, that would be awful!" said Carla. Her face wore an expression of shock.

"Why?" I asked, though I thought I knew what the answer would be.

"Because everyone would know."

"Know what?"

"Know that something is wrong with me—something awful. And that would be more than I could bear."

Carla was convinced she had to keep all other people believing she was calm, serene, adequate, stable, unruffled—in short, perfectly controlled. And not merely most of the time, but at *all* times. And it was this belief in the necessity of non-communication that made her relationships with others frequently tense and anxious.

The point I am making by telling you Carla's story is this: *Many people sincerely believe they must exert great effort to conceal what they really are, rather than reveal themselves to others. Furthermore, they believe that the result of revealing themselves to anyone else will always be disastrous.*

NOT "PIGGING OUT" ON ATTENTION

Nothing in this book should be interpreted to mean that people must talk endlessly about nothing but themselves. It is not a special virtue to focus attention on self. Self-revelation is not an exercise to boost the ego. I am not advocating that the subject of all conversation should be self, nor am I suggesting that self-adulation and self-glorification ought to make a comeback in Christian circles. The sort of conversation exemplified below is *not* what we're after:

> I'm the kind of guy when I get my feathers ruffled I don't mince words. So when this cop stopped me, I said, "And what's the problem?"
>
> And he said, "Sir," (he definitely called me "Sir") "you were going over the speed limit."
>
> "Well," I told him, "I was driving at exactly the same speed as the other traffic, so I'll take the matter to court if you try to give me a ticket."
>
> He could see I meant business—when I say something like that it's not an empty threat. I have a lawyer friend who told me, "Tom, any time you need me, just call. I'm great in traffic court, and I do know several people . . ." Anyway, I had this cop completely buffaloed. I knew it when he backed off and just gave me a warning. I don't take any guff from these guys.

We can hear similar boastful, attention-demanding "I's" in nearly any group having an ordinary conversation. The Christian, however, dead to self through the cross of Christ, has put aside such self-centered "pigging out" on attention. He now has a renewed self. He can still enjoy recognition and attention and find them reinforcing (as psychologists would put it), but he doesn't crave them desperately and they are not the aim of his life's activities.

It is no crime to say "I." It can even be valuable and loving to reveal the truth about your thoughts, beliefs, attitudes, opinions, and feelings to others. It is often very courageous and considerate to let someone else discover your innermost thoughts and feelings, and it is distortion (of truth and relationship) to be always on guard lest your true self be seen. It would be hard to find fault with such expressions as these:

> "I was greatly helped by the teaching you gave in our Bible study."
>
> "I have to admit that there are times when my anger gets away from me. I think it would help if you would pray with me."
>
> "I didn't like it when you lost your temper the other

day during our discussion."

"I love you."

"I really appreciate what you did for me."

"I seldom enjoy TV, but there was a show on last night that moved me so deeply I'd like to watch it again."

A COUPLE AVOIDING "I"

Let us tune in on a couple in dialogue. In this conversation both people show their fear of direct and truthful communication. Notice how frequently they substitute a question for a straight statement of the truth, and how hard both persons work to avoid saying "I."

Lara: Don't you think you ought to spend some time with the kids? They haven't seen their father for two weeks!

Bill: What's wrong with your eyes? Can't you see me having dinner with them every night? And what did I do Saturday afternoon—*all* afternoon?

Lara: Do you call taking Johnny to the dentist spending time with him? Don't you ever want to play ball with him like other fathers do with their sons?

Bill: What about two nights ago? You didn't see the shape George, next door, was in when he got home, did you? Would you rather have a husband like him? You want me to stop off for a few drinks after work like he does? He's one of those "other fathers" you think are so wonderful!

Lara: Speaking of getting home late, when are you going to start calling me when you work overtime? The other night you. . .

Not surprisingly, this discussion didn't get anywhere. By the time they reached this point, both Lara and Bill had forgotten the issue they were discussing and were busy firing salvos at each other, each trying to win the battle by annihilating the other. This couple's greatest hindrance to progress was, among other things, their studied avoidance of "I."

PRACTICE USING "I"

As people learn not to avoid the personal pronoun, "I," their speech usually becomes more direct and truthful. This chapter has shown that avoiding "I" is occasionally the result of a misbelief that the use of this word is somehow selfish and wrong. In fact, truthful expression about what a person wants and expects from others is often less selfish and more loving than circumlocutions.

Set yourself a goal for increasing the number of "I" statements in your conversation. Begin by noticing what sorts of substitutes you habitually use for "I" sentences. Do you say, "Don't you like detective stories?" when you really mean, "I like detective stories"? Perhaps you say, "You probably think. . ." when you mean, "I think. . ." Below are some more examples. Try changing them. Practice making "I" sentences out of them.

"Don't you think we're going to have a change in the weather?"

"Look at all the work we got done today."

"It would be nice if someone would consider me once in a while."

"That red coat doesn't look very good on you."

"After four years, college was finally completed and a job was found."

"It was fun being with you."

When you locate flaws such as these in your own conversation, practice changing your speech. Record how many simple, direct "I" statements you make in the next three days. Then try to double that number in the following three days. Soon, you will find your speech becoming more direct and truthful. Of course, you will want to guard against glorifying or glamorizing yourself while you are learning to use the word "I" more often. Remember, your purpose is telling the truth. You want to use the word "I" when that is what you really mean and when it is the legitimate, appropriate way to say what you really mean.

FOR REVIEW, PRAYER AND DISCUSSION

1. Why do some people avoid the use of the pronoun "I" whenever possible?
2. Did Jesus avoid this pronoun? See Matthew 3:14; 5:17ff.; Mark 13:30; Luke 21:3; John 17:24 as examples; there are many, many others.
3. Did Jesus avoid expressing his needs and wishes? See the passages listed above.
4. Did Jesus avoid expressing negative feelings? See Matthew 26:38; Mark 3:5; John 11:35.
5. Why do you think Carla (in this chapter) was so afraid to let others know she had a problem with anxiety?
6. Why do we want to learn the unabashed use of the pronoun "I"?
7. In what circumstances would it be most important to use "I" to reveal to another your thoughts and feelings?
8. Can you think of some bad consequences which might follow from not revealing your thoughts and feelings in some circumstances?

CHAPTER THREE

Attacking and Defending vs. Speaking the Truth in Love

Carlo never did keep his second appointment, or make any further effort to continue seeing a psychologist. In a sense, the referral by his physician was virtually certain to fail, since people with Carlo's set of symptoms never believe they need psychological help. With all their might they fight against believing it—because they *want* their illness.

Carlo was seeking abdominal surgery, and with consummate skill he made himself appear to have appendicitis. The attack he staged appeared critical. But his physician's skill was even greater than Carlo's ability as an actor. Noticing scars from previous surgeries, and being unable to find objective evidence of appendicitis, the physician carefully uncovered Carlo's bizarre medical history.

Carlo was diagnosed as having a *chronic factitious disorder* (an imaginary disease). Such a patient, though in perfect health, is often able to lie effectively enough to convince physicians that he is ill. The result is that he spends his entire life either in the hospital or trying to get admitted. And from his point of view, seeing a psychologist would only spell the defeat of his deepest desire—the desire to live out his life as a surgical patient.

Carlo and others with this very rare diagnosis want only to avoid the truth. They want to dodge the truth to such an extent that they are willing to risk all life's opportunities, expose themselves to hazardous surgical procedures and potent medications, and even mutilate their bodies—all in order to avoid the truth that they are healthy.

The disorder is sometimes called *Munchausen's syndrome* after a fabled character in German folklore, Baron Munchausen, the world's greatest liar. Munchausen, like these poor patients, loved to lie so much that he actually avoided the truth whenever he could. Shamming is a way of life for these folks.

Many people need to learn truthful speech for precisely the same reason: Shamming has become a way of life. They have learned to sham with their tongues so well they do it without thinking. They live with relationships horribly contorted by their avoidance of truth, and, like Carlo, think nothing of it. And, like Carlo, they frequently find themselves not wanting to change.

Perhaps reading the previous chapters has already convinced you that many of us need to change the way we talk; that, when compared with the standards of truth set forth in Scripture, our speech appears littered with devices for avoiding truth. While we are working at repentance and change in the particulars already discussed in this book, we can go on to identify a few more common devices most of us use to communicate while bypassing the truth.

DEFEND AND ATTACK AND AVOID THE TRUTH

Let's listen in on Lara and Bill, whom we met before, and note how their habits of defending and attacking destroy all possibility of truthful communication:

Lara: When are you going to fix that dripping faucet? I can't stand it any more.

Bill: Well, you don't give me a spare minute. You know what you made me do yesterday, don't you?

Lara: Made you? You *offered* to take Mother home after dinner. Then you say I *made* you do it. No matter how nicely I ask you to do anything, you find a way to start a fight, don't you?

Bill: You call it a fight when all I'm doing is explaining why I haven't fixed your faucet? You always expect me to do more than I can handle.

Lara: Expecting too much? Let me tell you something, Bill. You're not the one to talk! Look at the list of things you expect me to do—and you never thank me for any of them.

Once again, the original issue is forgotten. Lara and Bill are, at this point, so involved in attacking and defending that the dripping faucet is no longer important or even remembered. All that counts now is winning. Perhaps the whole process is Bill's self-rescue tactic. Since he has never learned to say, "I don't want to fix the faucet now," defending and attacking provide a reliable device by which Bill can escape from performing requests he doesn't know how to refuse. Truth becomes lost in the conversations between attacker and defender. People use attacking and defending to avoid saying what they truly mean, and/or to avoid hearing what someone else means and wants them to hear.

For instance, suppose that Marla, fresh from a class on truthful speech, and eager to try some of her new truth skills, goes home and says to Herbert, "I want you to know I didn't like the way you kept interrupting me at the party last night."

Herbert, an inveterate attacker, is quite likely to think that he has been attacked, and therefore must protect himself. To preserve his pride and avoid admitting that he may have thoughtlessly interrupted his wife at the party, he will defend himself by going on the offensive—and he thinks he hasn't a moment to lose.

So Marla can expect Herbert to respond like this:

"Well, if you ever got anything straight and gave people accurate information, I wouldn't have to interrupt you. Last night I had to clarify nearly everything you said."

How did Marla handle that? Well, if her class had progressed far enough she might have learned how to say the following truth in a loving but firm tone:

"Yes, I do understand that you thought I was inaccurate and that you needed to clarify things. But I still want you to know it hurt me to be interrupted. I'd like you to stop doing it."

And if Marla hadn't yet learned the rest of her lesson, she probably would have attacked right back, defending herself in the process:

"You didn't have to clarify *everything*. And while we're on the subject, you really fouled up the facts when you were telling Tom about the mileage you're getting with your new Honda. But I didn't correct you, did I?"

ATTACKING

Look at a few more examples of attack substituted for truth and love:

"I suppose you'll spend the whole day watching TV—again!"

"So you went to *another* luncheon! You do that full time, don't you?"

"This fish is cold—but I suppose I ought to be glad you cooked it at all."

As you can see from these examples, attack is untruthful because it covers up the admission that the attacker wants something. Furthermore, attack is unloving, because it invariably conveys to the other person a negative squelch. Attack says, indirectly and in ways particularly difficult to deal with, "You are bad, evil, no good, and worthless. I am upset and angry with you."

Often people attack each other when they don't know how else to express their desire for change or when they want to avoid the issue the other person is raising. Attackers believe they cannot afford to listen or admit any mistake. They believe that, no matter what, they must stave off the issue of changing their behavior. They seem to believe that to change their ways would harm them.

Herbert, instead of attacking, could, with the aid of the Spirit of God, have chosen to speak truthfully and lovingly: "You know, I did interrupt you frequently and I can understand that it didn't make you feel very good. I'm sorry I hurt your feelings." Such a loving, truthful response would have done Herbert's self-image no damage at all, while the attack he thought would rescue his pride actually led to a verbal battle which left him and Marla glowering at one another and ashamed of them-selves.

DEFENDING

Defending is another way of avoiding the truthful word "I" in interpersonal communication—and avoiding other truth issues as well. People commonly perceive themselves as having been attacked, even when they weren't. For instance, in the above example, Herbert thought Marla was attacking him, though she had merely told him of her hurt. So Herbert attacked back. Sometimes, retaliation is a device for personal defense when a person perceives someone else to be attacking him. And even if he doesn't necessarily think he's being attacked, he may put up a defense out of sheer habit or to avoid responding to a request he would rather not honor. Here are some examples:

She: Could we see a movie tonight?
He: I think I take you out plenty!

She: I would really like a car with more horsepower.
He: I didn't pick out this car. You did.

He: I'm so hungry I could eat a horse!
She: I certainly hope you don't expect me to go home and cook after you've made me walk all over town with you.

She: We need a new carpet in the living room. The dogs have practically ruined this one.
He: I didn't pick out those dogs, and nobody asked my opinion about the whole subject. I'm not about to buy a new carpet.

"I couldn't help it."

"You made me do it."

"Well, I wouldn't have done it that way, but I was forced into it by the children."

"What I did was perfectly reasonable, you know."

"I was just doing what you told me to do in the first place."

"Well, the other day, you did something just as bad or worse. Let me tell you about it!"

"If you think I'm bad, what about your brother? I don't think you paid any attention to the way he treated your sister-in-law, but I did! I suppose you think he's perfect!"

Like attacking, defending avoids the truth because it is usually designed to preserve the *status quo,* even at the cost of twisting the truth. The defender thinks, *Rather than work on change, I will put up a good defense for what I am or do already.* Or else, like the attacker, he seeks to preserve his pride by avoiding any admission of guilt or weakness.

Removing defensiveness from speech and replacing it with truth requires work. Truthful speech substitutes understanding and admission of fault where this is appropriate. Truthful speech omits defensive self-whitewashing. Below are some examples of truth substituted for the defenses listed earlier.

"I realize you'd enjoy seeing a movie tonight, and I know you've been in the house all day, but I don't want to go out tonight. Sorry."

"Yes, I know you'd like a more powerful automobile. Perhaps next time we buy a car we can make that one of the more important considerations."

"I'll bet you are hungry after shopping all day. I am too. But I don't want to cook dinner tonight after all this walking. I'd like to get dinner in a restaurant."

"You're right about the condition of the living room carpet— it's taken quite a beating. But I don't want to help pay for a new one. I want that to be your responsibility since you chose the dogs and they've damaged the rug."

PRACTICING TRUTH INSTEAD OF DEFENDING

In order to help you practice making truthful, loving, non-defensive responses, below are some statements—cues—to which an attacker/defender would probably respond with attack or defense. Construct a truthful and loving response for each one. And bear in mind that love does not require you to agree with the other person's notions and whims. It is perfectly all right to disagree and even to refuse his requests. Refusals can be made in truth and love. The cues may not always be models of truthful, loving speech; it is not necessary for others to be truthful and loving in order for you to learn these new skills.

1. You need a haircut.
2. I wish you'd hurry.
3. If you were a good Christian, you wouldn't talk that way.
4. I don't see why you never take me to the movies—like tonight.
5. You sure blew it when you made us move to this city.
6. This sure is a funny way you planned for us to celebrate Christmas.
7. Why on earth did you order tickets for these seats?
8. Why are we taking this route?

GROWING UP ATTACKED

I had a difficult time establishing therapeutic rapport with Becky, age 18. Her feelings seemed to get hurt no matter how carefully I avoided saying anything negative about her. For example, I ended one session without praying for her. I had prayed for her many times in previous sessions, so Becky assumed she had now done something to offend me, that I no longer cared for her, and that our relationship was probably ruined. At other times, Becky would spend entire weeks stewing over some gesture I had made—such as the raising of an eyebrow. To her, these things meant she had displeased me in some way and that I was upset with her for something she had said or done or failed to do.

Becky wanted to stop her treatment sessions, feeling she had done so badly in our relationship that I must be offended, frustrated, and angry with her. Her solution for this problem in her past relationships had been to pull out of them. Now it was crucial that she learn new ways of dealing with others. In my judgment, Becky had to stay in therapy at all costs.

Why did Becky think ordinary gestures, facial expressions, or inadvertent omissions meant I was attacking her or that I was irritated by her? We discovered the reason early. She had grown up being attacked.

Becky's poor mother, with so much hurt of her own to deal with, did not realize she was handling her pain by clobbering her daughter. Over the years Becky learned to expect criticism, even to interpret facial expressions and gestures as signifying criticism. Attack was her mother's stock in trade, and Becky learned to believe, unconsciously, that her behavior always irritated others and that they were therefore striking out at her for nearly everything she did.

Becky learned to avoid this pain by leaving a relationship as soon as it became uncomfortable, making excuses to the other person for avoiding the relationship. As a result of her moving away from others, she never confronted them with her feelings that she was being criticized, and never gave them an opportunity to confirm or deny her impressions that she had upset them. Meanwhile, by passively avoiding people who liked her and sought her company, she kept her fear level down, but also eventually alienated others until they did become irritated. When Becky discovered others no longer liked her, she believed her original notions had been confirmed. Thus she had shaped the course of her relationships into a vicious circle.

Sometimes people who have unusual difficulty with relationships have grown up attacked. Having a parent whose criticisms took the form of aggressive attack can create an abiding expectation that, whatever one does, it will result in attack by others and that others are going to attack sooner or later. Such persons may develop an attitude of perpetual defensiveness. Becky would often make a defense response even if she wasn't actually attacked because she always expected others to be on the attack.

DEFENDING WHEN YOU AREN'T ATTACKED

Some readers of this book may be defenders, even when not attacked. If you don't fit the bill, you may live with someone who does—or work under someone who does. Below are some examples. You may find they occur frequently in your speech or in that of someone you know.

George:	Oh, look, there's an oriole in our back yard!
Nina:	I know it's an oriole; you don't have to show off to me.
Cindy:	What movie would you like to see, honey?
Paul:	Why do you always make me pick the show?
Roommate #1:	You seem depressed. Feeling kind of down?
Roommate #2:	I can't help it! Get off my back, will you?
Janet:	Want some more pie, Rita?
Rita:	Yeah, sure, then you'll say I'm too fat!

Nina, Paul, Roommate #2, and Rita all share with Becky two underlying convictions: They believe they are being attacked because it's inevitable that others will try to put them down or show them up. They believe that they are inferior to others and that others will always act in a way to show off their superiority. They expect that any actions or words of others amount to criticism and attack, even when those actions or words appear innocuous. In addition, they believe that they must defend themselves to survive. They invariably tell themselves it is vital to defend.

> **Their two main misbeliefs are: (1) "I am surely being attacked," and (2) "I must always defend myself."**

LEARNING THE TRUTH ABOUT ATTACK AND DEFENSE

If you are a defender, you will have difficulty in relationships because of your long-held belief that others are attacking you. Learn now to tell yourself the truth about attack, as well as about the notion, possibly learned at your mother's knee, that you must always defend yourself. In Becky's case we worked out a plan for change.

After Becky had kept records for a week, logging each instance of defensive speech, as well as each instance of feeling attacked by someone (even if she didn't respond by defending), we studied the incidents she had logged. In none of them did it appear likely that she had actually been attacked; Becky was able to grasp that truth when she examined her log carefully with my help. She could also see that her defensive responses were damaging her relationships. And finally, Becky learned she had been failing to tell herself the truth in these interactions with others. She had thus spoken to others what was not true, and spoken it in fear rather than in love.

After Becky understood her misbeliefs ("I am being attacked" and "I must always defend myself"), we proceeded to stage two of our plan. Now we devised some self-directing self-talk which Becky memorized for use in interactions with others. She was to tell herself the following:

"Hold it, Becky. You're not being attacked. Scrap that defending response because it's based on lies and misbeliefs! Think a minute and give a response that is both truthful and loving."

In stage three Becky was to instruct herself, using her memorized speech, each time she was tempted to defend herself. She was to log the interactions in which this occurred so we would have a record of her progress.

Improvement was rapid. Becky had initially logged from eight to ten defending responses in each of her first weeks of record-keeping. After applying self-instruction, her first weekly total dropped to two defending responses. The next week, zero. And from then on, as long as we kept records, Becky was logging between zero and two defending responses per week.

Of course, Becky's relationships improved. No longer put off by her defending, other people warmed up to her as they never had before. Becky joyfully discovered trust, closeness, and deep affection. With her heart full of praise to God, Becky read and reread Ephesians 4.

After terminating her sessions, Becky entered college and

shared an apartment with roommates. It soon became evident that one of her roommates was an inveterate attacker.

One night Becky was studying her math assignment with her radio playing softly beside her. Suddenly Jo, the attacker, rose from her chair, stalked over to Becky's radio, and with evident anger and irritation shut it off.

"Do you mind?" said Jo with the sort of inflection that meant, "You really should have known that your radio was disturbing me. You're an insensitive person and you upset me."

"I was flabbergasted!" Becky told me later. "I hadn't been defending for so long, and I'd gotten so accustomed to telling myself that I wasn't being attacked, that at first I couldn't believe I was being attacked. But you'll be pleased with what I did. I told myself there was still no reason for me to defend. And I didn't.

"Instead I said, 'I can understand that my radio was disturbing you. And I don't mind a bit if you'd rather have it turned off. But from now on I would like you to tell me quietly if something I do is disturbing to you.' "

There were other similar confrontations with Jo, but Becky was able to handle most of them without defending. As a result her requests for Jo to stop attacking made an impression. Meanwhile, even on those occasions when Jo chose to attack, Becky was able to react effectively and calmly. The result was an enormous increase in Becky's feelings of adequacy and ability to cope.

KEEP A LOG

Perhaps you want to change your own untruthful speech and the misbeliefs which give rise to untruthful communication . with others. You may be an attacker or a defender, or for that matter, you may discover yourself in all of the miscommunication patterns identified in this book! You may not have known before reading this book the reasons for your chronic feelings of loneliness, your persistent sense of being misunderstood and "taken the wrong way."

If you want to change, if you find yourself saying, "I can see patterns of attacking and defending in me and/or in others around me," you will find it necessary to work very hard. So begin with prayer and make a commitment to God.

Then keep a log. Write down each incident in the category of things you have decided to work on. Keep a good record of every single incident for a week. This will give you a baseline measure of how often your untruthful behavior occurs. You'll be able to gather hard evidence of change in case the devil tries to tell you later that all your efforts are fruitless and that you are a hopeless case.

After keeping your log for a week, study it to find patterns of unloving or untruthful communication. Perhaps yours will be a problem of attacking or defending or both. Perhaps you'll discover some other patterns you'd like to change as you work through this book. Note carefully the beliefs which undergird your behavior. And analyze them carefully to determine which ones are misbeliefs.

Next, make up a set of self-instructions similar to Becky's and memorize them. They are now yours to use in your self-talk when episodes similar to those on your log occur in the future. You may even want to practice in your imagination. (Suppose that so-and-so has done or said such-and-such. Then give yourself your new self-instructions and invent a calm, truthful, effective response to use in reply.)

Finally, start applying your new patterns in actual relationships. This set of very basic steps can bring about enormous changes in your interpersonal behavior, and lead to positive improvement in relationships. Continue keeping your log so you can tally improvement.

Be sure to pray daily during this learning process. Ask especially that the Spirit of Truth will reveal to you the truth for each situation, as well as the truth you need to express to others. Just as important, pray for the gift of love to keep your truthful behavior focused toward the other person's good.

LIKE CARLO

The attacker or defender is very much like Carlo, the man you met at the beginning of this chapter. His Munchausen's syndrome, though very rarely encountered in medical practice, resembles conditions found much more frequently in daily life. Their habit patterns are like Carlo's in that they distort the truth.

The attacker is hiding the truth behind his attack. The truth he hates to speak out simply and plainly is his request, his wish, his straightforward statement of what he wants or how he feels. Similarly, the defender is too busy covering his supposed fault or weakness. He thus fails to notice or tell the truth about his reaction to the attack—whether real or imagined. Unlike Carlo, however, many who have these engrained habits and others like them are able to recognize what the truth is and to work on change.

Perhaps as you read on, you will discover other patterns of miscommunication which have crept into your repertoire. If you do, you may want to work toward change, toward the goal of this book: that you and other readers will tell each other the truth.

FOR REVIEW, PRAYER AND DISCUSSION

1. What is *chronic factitious disorder* and why does it resemble the miscommunicating speech of many people?
2. Make up three everyday examples of attacking and/or defending speech.
3. What does attack speech cover up? (What makes it untruthful?)
4. Now invent attacking/defending replies to the examples you created in question 2.
5. Finally, invent new and truthful self-instructions and then devise loving and truthful speeches to replace the examples you made up for questions 2 and 4.
6. Why do people sometimes erroneously perceive themselves being attacked?
7. Besides not telling the truth, both attackers and defenders are often trying to avoid having to _____ .
8. List the steps Becky went through to change her speech habits.
9. Would you like to change any of your own speech habits? If so, in prayer make a commitment to work systematically. Now begin by starting to keep your log.

CHAPTER FOUR

Manipulation by Guilt

Which of the following is sometimes—even slightly—true of you?

_____ Occasionally I enjoy giving orders.

_____ I feel good when I can talk someone else into following my example.

_____ Once in a while I like to know that *my* ideas are being carried out.

_____ I like to give advice.

_____ I wish my spouse (or relatives or close friends) would more often consider what I want.

_____ People should listen to me, and if they did, things would go better.

_____ I like to persuade my friends to do the same things I do— buy the same make of automobile, for example.

If you checked any of the items above, or (it happens quite often) if you checked nearly all of them, you will want to develop a better way of telling others what you desire, and at the same time learn to recognize their freedom to decide. You will want to learn to tell others the truth. If you denied all or most of the inventory items, you are probably hiding from yourself the fleshly pride of authority.[1] The flesh loves to run things. Of course, some people are so shy and diffident they never try di-

---

[1] See chapter four of *Why Do I Do What I Don't Want to Do* by William Backus and Marie Chapian, published by Bethany House Publishers, 1984.

rectly to tell others what to do, but even the shy and diffident would *like* to get their way. When they fear making a direct request, they will often resort to indirect methods for getting others to do what they want.

MANIPULATION

"Manipulate: to control or play upon by artful, unfair, or insidious means."[2] According to this Webster's definition manipulation is morally wrong. We are manipulating when we use these techniques to influence others.

Notice this does not mean it's wrong to get others to do something by saying, directly, what you want done. Neither does this mean no one should ever attempt to change others or persuade them to do things he wishes them to do. But manipulation, going beyond merely saying what is wanted, or beyond trying to persuade someone to change, is wrong. The manipulator thinks, *I can't just come right out and say what I want. John would never agree. So I have to figure out a way to make John do what I want him to do without directly stating what I desire.* Manipulation is usually fleshly and sinful because it is an attempt to control others without honesty or proper God-given authority.

Some people who use guilt to manipulate others also use guilt to control themselves, thus manipulating themselves as well. Those who are easily manipulated by others may also, in their self-talk, manipulate themselves. And they may be the more likely to try manipulating others by the same guilt-producing tactics. This chapter will show how telling the truth in love can help those who manipulate by guilt to become more straightforward by telling the truth.

"SHOULDS"

Do you have any friends who, without being asked, tell you their ideas about what you "should" do? Have you ever asked yourself what they really mean by all those "shoulds"? Maybe

---

[2]*Webster's New Collegiate Dictionary*

the following list will refresh your memory.

"You really should take your vacation in January. We do."
"You should get a better stereo; you ought to have one like ours."
"You should whack your kid once in a while. He'd behave better."
"You shouldn't refuse my requests unless you have a good reason."
"You shouldn't go anywhere without me."
"Know what you should do? You should get another car, then you'd have a second car when you need it."

On they go, "shoulding" you about everything.

Do you dislike it when people talk to you that way? Probably so, though you may not know exactly what it is that irritates you until you analyze what's actually happening.

OBLIGATION STATEMENTS

"Should" sentences put people under obligation. They are often used where no real obligation exists. Obligation statements are phrases which, by their structure, make someone feel under compulsion to do or feel something. If he doesn't do what he is obligated to do he feels guilt. When obligation statements are used and there is no actual obligation, he may feel guilty anyway, just because of the way the words affect him. People often use such statements—usually unintentionally—to make others do what they desire. They may thus be using guilt to manipulate people.

Here are more samples of obligation statements:

"You *should* read the editorial page more and the sports page less."
"You *ought* to bring home some flowers."
"You *must* try harder to remember when I ask you to stop at the grocery store."

All of the above sentences imply that the listener owes something, and therefore it is imperative that he does what the speaker wishes.

Though the Word of God says, "Owe no man anything, but to love one another" (Rom. 13:8), most people are easy targets for the feelings of guilt and obligation these "should" statements generate. They seem to forget they are freed from the law by the cross of Jesus Christ. This freedom from rules invented by men extends even to "laws" concocted by relatives or friends who are trying to manipulate.

JORDAN

Jordan is a person who was manipulated by the "shoulds" and "oughts" of others. A sitting duck for guilt blasts fired by others, he also shot himself full of guilt with "shoulds."

Jordan's conversations with me were larded with guilt-producing phrases: "I ought to have mowed the lawn on Friday, but I waited until Sunday. I am a lazy procrastinator," or, "I should have repaired the roof three months ago, but I kept letting it go. I don't know what's wrong with me!"

Not too surprisingly, Jordan was complaining of depression, nervousness, worrying, and a kind of psychological paralysis. He just couldn't get going. People with this feeling of leaden sluggishness are often full of obligation misbeliefs.

Soon it became clear that Jordan was simply reiterating the very same phrases his wife was using to control him. He made this easy for her because he was convinced he was an awful person, a "lazy, no good procrastinator." But under the surface, nestled right next to the wad of guilt in his heart, Jordan kept another wad of livid fury.

Jordan was out of touch with his anger which was hidden under guilt, but even though he was hiding it from himself, Jordan was paralyzed with rage. He was frustrated at being manipulated by obligation statements. And he did not know how to claim and live in the freedom he had in Jesus because he never recognized that he was free. So he was powerless to deal with the bondages of obligation with which others held him.

Jordan's log included the following obligation statements:

"You really ought to call your mother today. She hasn't heard from you for two days."

"You really must get a haircut—you look terrible."

"You've got to plaster that damaged spot in the bath-room ceiling, and you've got to do it this week."

"You must get that lawn mowed today."

"You should take Nancy to the park."

"Remember what you said to Joe this afternoon? The way you put it, he's probably going to be hurt. You shouldn't have used the words you used."

No one likes to be steered into doing things out of guilt and obligation. Yet people have frequently been trained to believe the notions Jordan harbored. That is why they try to manipu-late others with "shoulds." And it is why they control others with the same tactics.

Often this sort of talk works all too well to produce guilt and behavior changes (superficial though they are) in others. This will often arouse anger in the person being manipulated. It also may produce compliance, yes, but somewhere inside him-self the recipient will resent the attempt to manipulate him.

THE LEGALISTIC MISBELIEF

Obligation language results in miscommunication because it rises from the *legalistic misbelief:* "My life and most of my behaviors are a matter of obligation; of obeying laws, rules, and norms. There is little room for desires, wishes, and free choices. In fact, my desires are probably very bad, and it is selfish to have wishes."

The Apostle Paul, in his letter to the Galatians, teaches that the exact opposite is the truth: We are not under the law, but under the Spirit. Under the Holy Spirit we receive new desires from God who dwells within us. If we follow these God-gener-ated desires we exhibit behaviors which are the fruit of the Spirit. Our fruit-bearing behavior grows freely out of our new nature as children of God, and does not occur as a result of telling ourselves, "I must, I should, I have to . . ."

AN EXERCISE

Keep a log for several days of all the obligation statements others make to you. Stop when you hear someone tell you, "You ought to, you should, you must . . ." Make a note of what it is you are supposedly obligated to do. Or, if you are a person who uses such statements on yourself and others (and unfortunately, most of us are), keep in your log a record of your own "should" statements. Maybe you will want to record both the obligation statements others make to you and those you make to yourself and others. Unless you make this kind of effort you will have a difficult time changing behaviors which have become second nature to you.

Be sure to notice what you are obligating others or yourself to do. Notice also what others are binding you to do. You will often be startled when you observe the sorts of things we human beings thoughtlessly try to make ourselves or others to do as sacred duty and moral obligation.

One fact will probably surprise you: The examples in your log deal with things which are, most often, matters of liberty. No commands from God compel us to do them.

"SHOULDING" ONE ANOTHER

Often, two people will engage in mutual obligating. Their talk sounds like quotations from a rule book. Here is a sample:

She: Don't you think you should write to my mother and thank her for the cuff links she sent you?

He: I think you should do it—she's your mother. I write my folks—you should write yours.

She: Your parents have never sent me anything. I think they should give us personal gifts as my folks do—not all that junk for the house.

He: You should be glad my mom thinks of the things we need as a couple. Your folks never do. At least my folks realize I'm not made of money.

She: You certainly aren't! I guess my folks think you're earning a decent living so we can afford our own eggbeater. Shouldn't you turn off that TV for a while? It'll ruin your eyes.

He: Now that you mention it, I think we could buy our own

eggbeater if you weren't throwing money away on other things. You should spend less for groceries. Clothes, too. And stop running around so much. And, while we're talking about eyes, how about yours? I'm still paying for your old glasses, and now you want new ones!

TEN[10] COMMANDMENTS

God gave ten commandments. But we human beings have discovered how to multiply them—by using obligation statements inappropriately to put ourselves and others under the law. These statements make our wishes sound like God's commandments, putting others under obligation to perform for us. We create a social climate in which people are chafing under the burden of, not ten commandments made by God for our good, but ten-to-the-tenth-power commandments cooked up by others—with a lot more where those came from.

Study your log. Notice that most of the obligation statements are untrue. That is, there is no actual law on the books of heaven or earth which prescribes the actions urged on you—or those you have urged on others.

Look again at Jordan's log recorded earlier in this chapter. Not one of the ten commandments prescribes the duty of telephoning one's mother at least once every three days. Nor do the law books of government at any level reveal such an obligation. A moment's reflection on the fourth commandment shows no such requirement, since there are many, many ways a person might honor his parents without making daily phone calls. If Jordan's log were truthful, laws would exist somewhere demanding frequent haircuts, plastering, letter writing, lawn mowing, and visits to the park.

And even if such laws existed, obligation would not be the basic motive for Christian behavior. Remember, those who are in Christ have died to the law ("For I through the law died to the law, that I might live to God," Gal. 2:19, RSV). The person alive to God does what his new self loves to do because he desires only what pleases his Lord, not because he constantly thinks about rules, laws, requirements, and obligations. He doesn't lay such things on others, either.

Look again at your log of obligation statements. Write out for each one the words which make it untruthful for you, a person who in Christ Jesus is free from the law. Willingly extend the same freedom to others as well.

Incidentally, some of the things you have called "shoulds" might be good ideas for you to consider. They won't often be utterly "off the wall." Only the legalistic tone and the guilt motivation make them harmful and inappropriate.

REVISING OBLIGATION STATEMENTS

When you have finished keeping your log for several days, and reviewed it to note how obligation sentences are usually untrue, try rewriting them. Make them say something true. Replace the shoulds, oughts, and musts with words that do not imply that the behaviors involved are commanded by God.

Your rewritten sentences will sound very different from the old ones. They may resemble these:

"I would really appreciate it if you could fix the ceiling some time this week."

"Nancy has been asking to go to the park and I would like you to take her. Do you think you'd be willing to?"

"I want the lawn to look good for our company tomorrow and I'd like you to mow it today. Will you?"

"I want to call Mom and let her know how much I care about her. It's been a couple of weeks since she's heard from me, and I don't want her to worry."

Notice that "I want you to," "I would like you to," "I want," and "I like" replace the obligation statements. That is because the truth behind most obligation statements is really a wish or desire of the speaker. Obligation statements cloak these desires in the guise of requirements or commandments.

Telling each other the truth means admitting we are merely voicing our wishes, not the eternal will of God, when we make everyday requests of one another. It may also mean translating the obligation statements of others so that we don't let them trap us into a network of guilt.

Below is a table of "should" statements paired with their

truthful revisions. Practice revising your "should" statements in the same way.

UNTRUE "SHOULDS"	TRUE "WISHES" AND "WANTS"
1. You should take the time to thank me once in a while for all I do for you.	1. I would really feel good if you were to tell me you appreciate some of the things I do for you.
2. You must get ready now; we just can't be late again.	2. I want to be at this party on time; will you please be ready by a quarter to five?
3. You ought to brush your teeth two or three times a day to keep your breath fresh.	3. I don't like to kiss you when your breath isn't fresh. I wish you would brush your teeth more often. Would you be willing to?
4. You ought to turn off that TV and get outside and rake those leaves up. Randy, next door, finished his lawn this morning!	4. Our lawn is covered with leaves and I don't like the way it looks. I feel embarrassed because our neighbor's lawn is clean and ours isn't. It would really please me if you'd rake them up today. Will you?

Notice how frequently the word "I" is used in the above statements. If you are going to tell others the truth, you will have to admit it when the purpose of your speaking is to gratify a wish or desire of your own. And, despite what you may have been led to believe, there is nothing wrong with having and expressing wishes. There is, however, something wrong with cloaking them in the guise of laws and commandments, as if heavenly authority were always on your side.

There is a need for "should" language. It is perfectly appropriate when it refers to true duty and obligation. If God has commanded something it is usually truthful, straightforward, and loving to say such things as:

"You should love your neighbor as yourself."
"You must obey the traffic light."
"You must not steal your neighbor's peaches."
"You ought not get drunk and drive a car."

But notice that these statements are not mere disguises for some friend's wishes. They are true obligations, leveled by God or by God-instituted authority.

FREEDOM FROM MANIPULATION

If you have a problem with easily-aroused guilt, you will want to use this chapter to gain freedom from the bondage of being readily manipulated. Do others "lay a guilt trip" on you rather easily and thereby manipulate you or, failing that, leave you feeling guilty, frustrated, and angry? Claim your freedom in Christ, the freedom expressed in Romans 13:8 ("Owe no man anything, but to love one another"), and tell yourself the truth about the real meaning of most of the obligation statements others direct toward you. Remind yourself repeatedly, "That person is really only expressing his wishes and desires, and I am not obligated to fulfill them!"

Perhaps you are frequently nagged by a person who tries to put you under guilt and obligation with such phrases as, "You know, you really should hang up your own towel and washcloth instead of expecting me to do it for you." If so, you will want to learn to translate the speaker's "shoulds" into more appropriate language and rephrase his request for him. Even if he just acknowledges your way of saying it, communication between you will be improved.

Here is an example of "translating":

Obligator: Don't you think you should rake the lawn this afternoon? We're having company tomorrow, you know.

You: You're saying you'd like me to rake the lawn so you'll feel good about the way our house looks when the guests come tomorrow?

Obligator: Yeah, well—yeah. I would appreciate it.

Once the other person's obligation statement has been translated into an expression of his wishes, you are free to express your wishes in the matter too, and together you can work out a solution if your desires conflict. Such a resolution is hardly possible if one person insists that his desires are tantamount to the law of God.

Remember, in Christ you are free from the law. And so is the other guy! Count on the truth-telling help of the Spirit of God!

In this chapter we have focused on the guilt-producing use of "shoulds, oughts, and musts." There are many other common devices for generating guilt and manipulating by means of guilt, and in future chapters we will learn about them and how to deal with them, as well as how to stop using these tactics.

FOR REVIEW, PRAYER AND DISCUSSION

1. Is it wrong to want, sometimes, to change another person's behavior?
2. What is manipulation?
3. Differentiate between manipulation and legitimate efforts to get another person to change.
4. What three words are often used by manipulators to generate guilt motivation?
5. Why are those words usually not appropriate?
6. Amy, a young college student, thought she was obligated to do anything anyone else wanted her to do. What would you say to that? (See Romans 13:8.)
7. Why do you think Jordan, in this chapter, was complaining of painful feelings?
8. What is the legalistic misbelief?
9. Now give the truth to counter the misbelief in question eight.
10. When are obligation terms appropriate?
11. The truthful rephrasing of most obligation statements begins with "I want you to . . ." or "I would like you to . . ." Make up an obligation statement and then rephrase it in truthful terms, beginning with one of these phrases.
12. What is one suggested way to deal with another person who habitually uses obligation statements instead of statements expressing his wishes (which would be the truth)?

CHAPTER FIVE

Ask and It Shall Be Given You—How to Make Requests

"The situation is so desperate I'm willing to try anything!"
Dawn could hardly pull herself together to tell me what she was weeping about. She had come to the psychologist without believing he could do much; but shaken down to the soles of her feet, she was willing to play a long shot.

"I thought my marriage was solid!" she sobbed, tearing sheet after sheet out of the tissue box and daubing at her tears with long, inaccurate swipes.

Just four days before Dawn's first visit her husband, Trent, had told her he no longer loved her. He was taking extraordinary delight in talking to a woman who worked at the desk next to his. In fact, Trent suspected he might be in love with the other woman. She was, he said, especially warm and understanding in a way he had never before experienced.

Trent's announcement had almost destroyed Dawn. Though there had been no physical affection between Trent and the other woman, his relationship with her seemed closer and more mutually empathetic than his relationship with Dawn had ever been.

A fresh flood of tears and some more blotting provided an opening for me to ask, "What did you say when Trent told you about his feelings?"

"I asked him how he could possibly do such an awful thing and then *tell* me about it." Dawn pulled herself together so she could continue the interview.

"You asked him questions?"

"Of course! I asked him how he could dream of treating me this way. I asked him what I had done to deserve it. I asked him what fault he could find with anything in our marriage."

"Were you satisfied with Trent's answers?"

"What do you mean?"

"Did Trent's answers to your questions help to resolve the problem between you? And did you feel relieved?"

"Of course not! I just felt more angry and upset every time he opened his mouth!"

"Sometimes we ask questions when it would really be more truthful and appropriate to express our own feelings and desires," I replied. "It sounds, Dawn, as if you never even thought of telling Trent how you felt and what you wanted him to do under the circumstances. Instead, you asked questions."

"That's ridiculous! He knows how I feel—or he ought to. If he had any sensitivity whatever, he'd realize how upset all this was bound to make me."

Dawn was becoming irritated. She seemed incredulous that I should even suggest she could do something far more effective in her communication with Trent. She thought it logical to subject her erring husband to a battery of questions.

A HOME WHERE NOBODY MADE REQUESTS

It gradually became clear that Dawn had been raised in a home where conversations typically contained more questions than a quiz show. Sometimes the people in her home conversed without questions. Occasionally they narrated experiences and shared some feelings about life outside the home. But, when it came to their feelings about one another, Dawn's family resorted to questions. And when it came to communicating their own wishes to one another, they scored zero. They used questions and circumlocutions instead. They talked around the subject, hoping others would "get the hint"—or else ask one another for explanations.

So Dawn did what she had learned to do: She communicated indirectly. Rather than tell others her needs, she asked questions and dropped hints.

When the first interview had ended I knew what had blocked the way to closeness between Dawn and Trent. I wasn't sure yet how Trent dealt with the truth about his own needs and wants, but it was clear as a sunny day in January that Dawn rarely said what she wanted. Like most of us, she had learned much from the role models she had grown up with—her parents. Because they had always avoided direct communication about their wishes, she too avoided telling others the truth about her desires. She used the tactics of questioning and hinting. Such tactics produced many negative byproducts destructive to Dawn's marriage. Dawn needed to learn to tell the truth about her wishes, to make requests.

I formulated quickly the treatment plan for Dawn. I was to provide her with a new role model, and to teach her to express her wants. Over and over we role-played conversations. Dawn learned not to say things such as, "Why don't you ever tell me you love me?" She learned how to say, instead, "I want you to tell me you love me more often, please."

With effort Dawn changed her behavior. She learned to express her wishes and desires to Trent openly and directly.

Admittedly, there were some discussions between Dawn and me about the appropriateness of all this. I encourage clients to discuss their thoughts, feelings, and wishes for their therapy. Dawn did just that.

Like many other people, Dawn had (erroneously) come to believe it was somehow wrong to say the words, "I want . . . I want you to . . . I don't want . . . I don't want you to . . . I would like . . . I wouldn't like. . . ." To Dawn, such expressions were transparent evidence that the speaker was selfish.

Dawn believed that a truly spiritual person would never give any expression to his own wants, but would, instead, be interested only in the wants, needs and feelings of others. I had to show her that this notion was both unbiblical and unreasonable, a tactic of the enemy to fog human communication and produce trouble. Finally she began to see that this distortion of the meaning of selfishness and self-giving was playing a major role in the deterioration of her relationship with Trent.

Trent was now ready to come in at my request. He expressed interest in working on his marriage when he discovered that the procedure would involve, not long hours of recounting every detail out of the past history of the relationship, but training in how to be close and honest with the woman he had married.

I wasn't surprised to learn that Trent routinely avoided telling Dawn or anyone else what he wanted them to do. After both Trent and Dawn were taught to express their wishes directly and to handle each other's direct expressions, they were given six sessions of training in solving their problems with the truth.

Trent discontinued his conversations with the other woman, preferring to develop closeness with Dawn. Today, their marriage is solid because they learned how to reach one another with the truth.

IS IT WRONG TO SAY, "I WANT"?

A session of family therapy was in progress. The topic, raised by Harry, was family efforts to cope with Beverly's premenstrual syndrome (pms) behavior.

I asked Beverly a few questions about her tolerance for medications which her physician had suggested. Suddenly she burst into tears and shouted, "Why is the problem always me? Why are we talking about me all the time? Why can't we once in a while talk about somebody else? I can't stand this!"

Everyone in the room was startled, including me.

"Beverly," I asked, "do you want us to stop discussing your pms now?"

"I don't see why I'm always made to take the blame for everything!" Beverly shouted through her tears, as she worked up to a real tantrum.

"Just tell us your wishes, Beverly," I said, "and please do it without shouting."

Beverly continued to yell for a while, then finally calmed down and allowed the session to progress. She had made one thing startlingly clear: She found it easier to lose her cool, cry, and shout generalities than simply to say, "I want you to stop talking about my pms for now."

Beverly, like many readers of this book, had been taught it is not nice to say, "I want." She was sure that to directly express her wishes and likes was somehow selfish. As a result, she had developed a habit of getting what she wanted by temper tantrums. Though she was ashamed of them and felt defeated after each one, they enabled her to avoid saying, "I want." Until this key was found, she had prayed and made resolutions to no avail. The tantrums seemed bigger than she was. After she learned to express her wants truthfully, she gained victory over the tantrums.

Those who never say, "I would like you to . . ." or "I want . . ." usually learn some other, more destructive tactics for obtaining fulfillment of their wishes and needs. Temper tantrums, putdowns, hinting, questioning, generating guilt, door slamming, and pouting—all are methods for getting one's way without saying, "I want."

I DON'T WANT TO *MAKE* HIM DO IT

Some people believe that the mere expression of a direct wish to another person "forces" that person to comply. When I first try to teach them to make a direct request they argue, "I don't want him to feel he *has* to do it for me." Of course it would be evil and selfish to force or manipulate another against his will. But does speaking the truth actually involve the use of force? Of course not. No one is forced or compelled by a simple request. We all have as much right to refuse requests as to make them.

NOTE: Later this book will discuss the need most people have to learn to refuse requests, to say no. If a person is free to make his requests known to another, he is also free to turn another down. The person who automatically does whatever another person asks must learn to discriminate. Love and the Holy Spirit are the keys to knowing when the right response is to honor a request and when to say no. But clearly, no one is forced or compelled by a request.

Dawn objected to the idea that she should "come right out and ask" directly for what she wanted. "I thought the desires and wants we have come from the sinful old self and are supposed to be crucified," she argued.

She was partially right, "For you have died, and your life is hid with Christ in God." However, ". . . if any one is in Christ, he is a new creation; the old has passed away, behold, the new has come" (Col. 3:3; 2 Cor. 5:17, RSV). "New" includes new desires. But the enemy has a demonic program for trying to return a believer to his old selfish ways. A Christian certainly has the capacity to be selfish, but he is now free to be unselfish. And the new nature does have desires which can be fulfilled unselfishly.

Many wants and desires are basic needs (e.g., Jesus' thirst at the well in Samaria), or even Spirit-given drives, wishes, and feelings of the new man. Normally, therefore, it is truthful (and loving) for a person to say plainly what he wants from another. By developing discernment a person will be able to hear the Word of God and the Spirit of Truth so he can sift out selfish wants from legitimate desires.

Some people don't speak directly of their wants because they avoid the pronoun "I." (See chapter 2.) They believe it is selfish or in bad taste to speak of themselves. They may even avoid saying "I" to God! But there is a huge difference between using the personal pronoun to express legitimate wishes and loading conversation with "I's" all meant to laud self and give glory to the ego.

If you avoid using the word "I," especially to express your wants and wishes directly, you can set a goal to increase your awareness of your own speech habits and to increase your directness and honesty. Set a week-long goal of deliberately saying to someone, in at least three instances per day, "I want you to . . ." or "I would like you to . . ." or "I don't want . . ." or "I don't like. . . ." In each instance write down what you said, what the other person said in response, and what the result was.

At the end of the week look over the log you have kept and evaluate it in the light of Scripture. You should discover that your truthful speech is less selfish and sinful than the old devices you substituted for truthfulness. You might want to set another goal for subsequent weeks, continuing until the new speech pattern feels natural to you.

THE TROUBLE IS YOU DON'T ASK

The principle of asking directly is well-established in Scripture. Jesus taught, "Ask, and it will be given you; seek, and you will find; knock, and it will be opened to you. For every one who asks receives, and he who seeks finds, and to him who knocks it will be opened" (Luke 11:9, 10).

Paul, like Jesus, advocates direct requests to God. He exhorts the Philippians, "Have no anxiety about anything, but in everything by prayer and supplication with thanksgiving let your requests be made known to God" (Phil. 4:6, RSV).

The letter of James in the New Testament could be used as a textbook for a course in Christian communication. "You do not have, because you do not ask" (James 4:2, RSV), states the case succinctly. Although in this verse James is referring to communication with the Heavenly Father, he is also discussing troubled relationships. And he is saying that some of the troubles in his readers' relationships with God are due to failure to ask directly for things. In the same way that people need to speak openly to God they need to deal openly with one another.

If direct, honest expression enhances a person's relationship with the Holy Creator of heaven and earth, it is bound to enhance his relationships with brothers and sisters in the family of God. So, when someone does not receive from others the consideration, the love, the help, and the cooperation he deems appropriate, it is often the case that "he does not have because he does not ask."

Jesus expressed His wants directly. Consider the following examples:

"[I want you to] follow me and I will make you become fishers of men" (Mark 1:17, RSV).

"I will [I want to]; be clean" (Mark 1:41, RSV).

"If anyone says to you, 'Why are you doing this?' say, 'The Lord has need of [wants] it. . .' " (Mark 11:3, RSV).

"[I want you to] Give me a drink" (John 4:7, RSV).

"Father, I desire [want]; that they also, whom thou hast given me, may be with me where I am. . ." (John 17:24, RSV).

I am not saying that every whim should be expressed to other persons. There are times when it is not appropriate to ask. Sometimes ordinary politeness and good etiquette govern whether or not to ask. For instance, if someone is invited to dinner and his host serves hamburger, it would not be especially cool or appropriate to say, "Pardon me, but if it wouldn't be too much trouble for you, I'd like you to prepare a T-bone steak for me." Neither would it be right to ask another person to do wrong: "I want you to commit larceny with me," or "Let's commit adultery together," are obviously wrong requests.

James and John's mother, Salome, brought a wrong request to Jesus: "I want my boys to be top men (next to you, of course, Lord) when you come into the kingdom. I just want them to be first." Jesus rebuked her and the boys for asking such a thing (but He did not rebuke them for making a direct request), then taught them what true greatness in the Kingdom would mean— sacrifice and service for others, even to the point of death. Greatness is not, as they had thought, holding powerful, honor-laden positions.

WHAT PEOPLE DO INSTEAD OF ASKING

What do people do instead of coming right out and asking for what they want? Some prefer to do just about *anything*. They are so bent on avoiding direct requests, they will simply go without rather than ask. It's rather common to hear words such as these:

> "I'm not going to ask him for it. He should know that it's important to me. If he loved me, he would do it automatically. What an insensitive person he is, not to have noticed! No sir, Doc, I'd rather forget about it than come right out and ask a klutz like him!"

There is a problem with those who say, "I'd rather do without than ask." They most often don't merely do without. They instead become frustrated. Or irritated. When the other person doesn't automatically sense and anticipate their desires they feel aggravated. They may try to hide their feelings, but generally that doesn't work and they resort to indirect measures to get even.

Those measures often consist of *passive-aggressive tactics*. Showing anger and disappointment through procrastination, stubbornness, dawdling, inefficiency, and "forgetfulness" is passive and ineffective. He keeps forgetting to fix her favorite chair. She burns the beans she knows he loves. He forgets to pick up her package at the drug store. She neglects putting enough starch in his shirts. All these are pretty worthless communication devices, yet people use them to tell others they are upset because they did not get what they wanted—but wouldn't ask for.

A common passive-aggressive measure is *crying*. Although genuine tears are a normal emotional outlet, some crying is an indirect expression of bitterness or anger. Crying is a common symptom among those who pride themselves in doing without rather than asking for what they want. The following example demonstrates this.

Dave often finds Nelda weeping softly. Over the years they have developed their routine so that what happens next is as clear to Dave as if they were reading a script. He is to ask what is wrong. The script calls for her to shrug her shoulders and sob, "Nothing!"

With that answer Dave knows what he has suspected: There is trouble. He has done something. *What*, he wonders, *could it be?* He probes again and Nelda runs from the room to throw herself onto her bed. Dave follows her, begging. All he wants to know is what on earth he has done.

After Nelda determines that Dave has suffered almost enough she reveals the reason for her tears. Punctuating her narrative with sobs, Nelda tells how she has noticed from her kitchen window that Lew, across the street, brings home flowers every Friday afternoon. To her the conclusion is inescapable: Lew must genuinely love his wife.

"But—" she shrieks, "as long as we've been married, you've never brought me flowers unless it was some special occasion!" Nelda wants flowers but won't ask because she has persuaded herself that Dave must bring them spontaneously if the flowers are to prove he truly loves her.

Dave soon becomes irritated and a full-scale battle erupts, ruining the weekend for this couple. But even worse, Nelda's substitution of passive-aggression for direct asking becomes more frequent. And unless the process is checked it will result in Dave's developing a wary approach to life. He will walk, uncomfortably, on eggs, around his wife. He will believe that he simply cannot afford the punishment he would receive if he were to be truly honest with her. And she will feel even more closed out and unloved.

Such tactics merely destroy. Men and women who pride themselves on not asking, meanwhile substituting anger and self-deception, need to see clearly that the "anger of man does not work the righteousness of God" (James 1:20, RSV), nor does it lead to improved relationships. Rather the "anger of man," repeatedly and chronically substituted for plain asking, kills human closeness and love.

Some people who would rather "do without" resort to *hinting*. Look at the following examples:

"Don't you think it's a little cold in here?" means "Please close the window."

"What would you like for dinner, hot dogs?" means "I'm hungry for hot dogs and I'd like you to get some for dinner tonight."

"Don't you think your hair is a little long?" means "I'd like for you to get a haircut today."

"Don't you just feel like redecorating the living room with completely new wallpaper and furniture—a fresh color scheme?" means "I want to buy new wallpaper and furniture for the living room. What do you say to that?"

"Not one person at church has ever offered to pray with me!" may mean "I would like for you to pray with me."

A patient was, unavoidably, kept waiting until fifteen minutes after the hour of his appointment. When he was finally ushered into the consulting room, he pointed to his watch before sitting down, a frozen smile on his face, and said, "It's two-fifteen."

"So what?" the therapist replied, hoping the patient would express his feelings and wishes directly.

"It's a quarter after two," the client replied, his face still frozen in a smile which bared his teeth. This man was still hoping that his hinting, his indirect communication, would bring the therapist to apologize for keeping him waiting. He wanted all this to occur without his having to express himself directly. But the therapist wouldn't buy it.

"What of it?" asked the therapist.

Finally, the patient had no choice but to say directly that he was angry and upset because he believed he would not get the time he had paid for.

"You'll get all the time you paid for," the therapist replied. "But you'll get more than that. I want to teach you how to deal with me and others when you want something. If you will learn today how to do that, then start practicing it, you won't feel as helpless, upset and angry as you felt just now. And you will be able to do something effective when you are bothered by the actions of others."

For the remainder of that hour, the therapist modeled and the patient imitated. He learned, among other things, how he could come into the consulting room, sit down, and say, "I want to ask you to give me the fifty minutes I have coming. I notice we are fifteen minutes late getting started, and I don't want to miss out on that much of our time together." He also learned to wear a serious expression rather than a meaningless grin when he wanted to deal with something seriously.

Building on this single episode, the patient began to practice dealing with other people by expressing himself directly. He drew closer to people with whom he worked. His perpetual frustration and resentment toward others diminished. His formerly high blood pressure readings approached normal. He began to spend his hours in bed sleeping instead of tossing and thinking about what he should have said to others or how he could get even with them.

"HE SHOULD DO IT WITHOUT BEING TOLD"

Rather than make direct requests of others, some people tell themselves that others should do the things expected of them without being told. They believe others should automatically perform according to their expectations. They insist that the world should conform to their notions of what ought to be. Thus they seek to impose a burden of legalistic obligation on others just so they won't have to take the trouble to ask directly.

Remember Dawn, whose problem was described at the beginning of this chapter? When I first tried to get her to tell Trent what she wanted, she argued vehemently: "Trent should know, without being told, that a woman needs affection and not just sex. And he should work out little ways to show his love for me without my having to spell them out for him. That spoils it. Other men take their wives out—and not just to prayer meetings either. I don't see why Trent couldn't think of such things himself. He really should!"

Dawn was eloquent on the subject of her belief about what Trent should do if he wanted to be a first-class husband. In a way she was right—it is awfully nice when somebody spontaneously brings gifts, does favors, goes out of his way to show affection, and exerts himself to please. Just because it's nice, however, doesn't make it obligatory. Yet many people exhibit a set of misbeliefs which far exceed this. For instance:

"Because it's nice when people do things I like, and especially nice if they do them spontaneously, it follows that others must please me, and must do so without being asked."

"If I have to tell another person what I want, getting it can't be worthwhile."

"To signify genuine love for me, others should change the way I want them to—but it should not be necessary for me to request the change. If I have to ask, our relationship is clearly awful and the other person obviously doesn't love me."

These statements reflect the Spontaneity Misbelief:

> **Spontaneity Misbelief:**
> **"I shouldn't have to ask. If I have to ask it ruins everything."**

If such beliefs are allowed to flourish and govern behavior

in relationships, they will destroy closeness and prevent genuine progress. Therefore it is important to learn to make requests.

Here are some reasons for learning to make requests:

1. *Making a sincere request is speaking the truth in love.* To ask, "Are you cold?" when you really mean, "I would like you to close the window" is indirect and beside the point. And because, through such communication, others are hurt, relationships are damaged, families are broken, and strife is generated, indirection can be unloving as well as untruthful.

2. *If you want a close relationship, learn to make requests.* No relationship can be close where significant desires are perpetually hidden. Two people may be close in physical distance, but the habit of not making requests erects a barrier to closeness of relationship.

3. *When another person's behavior bothers you, it is important to make requests.* Acting stoic may seem at first to be the Christian way. But a stiff upper lip when you seriously suffer from what someone else is doing may only make you cross and angry in the long run. Jesus spoke up when He was hurt by someone else. At His trial He was struck in the face. He did not quietly accept this, but spoke up, saying, in essence, "Please stop striking me or bring a witness to testify that I deserve punishment. Your behavior is violating my rights and I want it to stop" (John 18:22, 23). (You may think I am taking liberties with the text, but I believe this is the precise meaning of Jesus' words to the guard who struck him, as reported by the evangelist. Apparently there was no further trouble with this guard.)

Sometimes such simple requests are more effective than you think they will be. A professor, known for his sharp, sarcastic lashing out had his college classes frozen with fear. He was known for an acid tongue with which he etched emotional scars on hapless students. One day he began verbally immolating a young woman, right in front of the class. She interrupted with a calm "Please talk to me nicely." What could the professor do? He could not complain that she had been impertinent, and she certainly wasn't weakly inviting more scorn. For the remainder of the quarter he carefully refrained from lambasting the girl who had the courage to make a simple, truthful, dignified request. In fact, the man's demeanor improved toward the entire class.

4. *When you stop construing your requests as obligations you will be more comfortable making requests of others.* A young woman said, "Marge asked me to go to the movies last night. I couldn't think of an excuse, so I had to go." Repeatedly people tell me, "I didn't come right out and ask him because I didn't want to make him feel he had to do it." Aside from our duty to obey God-ordained authorities, we are free to deny or assent to the requests of others. Christian liberty means that we "owe no man any thing" (Rom. 13:8). Love may react to a request with compliance, refusal, or an alternative offer.

LEARNING TO MAKE REQUESTS

Here are the phrases you have to become comfortable with:
"I want."
"I don't want."
"I like."
"I don't like."
"I would like you to."
"I would not like you to."
"I would like."
"I would not like."
"Will you please?"
"Would you be willing to?"

Read the above phrases aloud several times until you become comfortable saying them. Many people have spent a lifetime avoiding such expressions. They need to become desensitized to them with practice.

Now rework the following statements, changing them into sentences which use the word "I" appropriately to express wishes:

Don't you think you should wipe your feet before you step on my clean floor?

Why don't you ever take me with you to your church?

Wouldn't you rather see a movie than go to a play?

You always have to make me wait for you or you're not happy!

Would you like to go for a walk with me?

Can't you quit insulting me?

It sure is cold in here since you opened that window.

You could pass the food to somebody else instead of just sitting there stuffing your face!

Begin introducing the above phrases into your conversation by taking the following steps:

Step 1: During the next three days, keep a log of your use of the direct request phrases in conversations. Don't try yet to increase their frequency, just note them down and note when and with whom you use them. If you should find yourself using any other phrases with identical meaning, log them too (e.g., "It would please me very much if you were to . . .").

After three days of careful tracking and logging, total up the number of occasions on which you used any of these phrases and divide by three. That will give you an average daily rate. This is sometimes called a base rate. If your base rate is three it means you use direct request phrases three times a day.

Step 2: Determine that over the following three days, you will increase your base rate. You may decide to increase it by one or two, or even more. Deliberately create opportunities to use request phrases. Keep careful notes on when and with whom and with what results you made your requests.

Step 3: Continue practicing these phrases, gradually training yourself always to make direct requests. Be sensitive to your old habits of indirection trying to come back. Remind yourself of the truth and combat your misbeliefs when they crop up.

Be sure to note changes in your own feelings and in the improvement in quality of your relationships. Look for increased freedom and joy, greater closeness to others in the Body of Christ, decreased anger in yourself, less friction and abrasiveness between yourself and others.

You may find it difficult to practice these principles. "I'd rather take a beating than ask," some people say. But by facing your fear and reluctance, and by patient practice, you can learn to ask in truth and love.

SOME EXAMPLES: RIGHT AND WRONG

Here are some examples from conversations in everyday situations. In each one you will find a concrete instance in which requests are made. You may want to use these examples as models for your own program of change.

Example 1: A Secretary Makes a Request. Imagine you are a secretary. You have just squirmed through a staff meeting in which your boss criticized you in front of the entire office staff. The criticism was sarcastic, caustic. You want to do something because this pattern has been occurring frequently. How will you handle your problem?

The *wrong* way to handle the problem:

You: I'll type this letter the best I can. I have had a lot of pressure lately.

Boss: Pressure's part of life. Get that out by noon, will you?

You: If I can.

Boss: I don't know what's wrong with you. Your attitude had better improve.

You: Well, if there were a little more appreciation and a little less criticism in this office—

Boss: If you don't like it here, you can look for another job, you know.

You: I know. Maybe I will.

The *right* way to handle the problem (after making an appointment to talk):

You: I'm having some problems with my feelings about the staff meeting yesterday—I was very embarrassed when you made a point of discussing my typing errors in front of everyone.

Boss: I didn't mean to embarrass you. It's just that so many errors bother me.

You: I know you like letters typed perfectly, and I don't blame you. I'm going to take extra trouble to proofread. But I would like you to tell me privately if you have criticisms. It would help me a lot.

Boss: Sure, I can do that. I guess I wouldn't like to be chewed out in public either. Thanks for talking to me about it.

Example 2: Making a Request of a Teen-ager. Angie, age 15, has been leaving her room a mess. Her mother wants her to keep it clean. Angie has just come down for breakfast before school.

The *wrong* way to handle the problem:

Mom: You're getting up later every day. You have to take time to eat your breakfast. Now you eat every bit of that oatmeal before the bus comes!

Angie: I don't like oatmeal. And I'm in a hurry.

Mom: You're always in a hurry. And that room of yours! What a pig pen! I don't know how you can stand the mess.

Angie: Get off my case, Mom, will you? I cleaned my room Saturday. And anyway, what about Buz? Have you looked at his room lately? Why don't you ever bug him? It's always me you pick on.

Mom: Buz has a paper route—he can't always clean his room.

Angie: You always stick up for him.

Mom: No, I don't!

The *right* way to handle the problem:

Mom: Good morning, Angie!

Angie: Hi.

Mom: I'd like to discuss something with you. It might take about ten minutes. Is this a good time for you?

Angie: No, Mom, it isn't. I have to eat and run. How about after school?

Mom: Fine. Will you be home about four o'clock?

(Later that afternoon they sit together in the kitchen.)

Mom: I want to work out something with you about keeping your room clean. I'm really uncomfortable when your bed isn't made and clothes are lying all over the floor. I'd like you to plan a way to keep it clean.

Angie: I can understand it bugs you when my room is a mess. You want me to make the bed every morning?

Mom: And pick up your clothes. Then once a week, I'd like you to dust and vacuum your room, change the bed, and wash, dry, and put away your sheets. Could you work that out?

Angie: I'd have to get up five minutes earlier. I've been meaning to do that anyway. Sure, Mom, I can give it a try.

GUARD YOUR MOTIVES

The goal of this chapter is learning to make requests, *not getting your way*. Other people may refuse your requests. Often, this is their right. Nothing in this chapter is meant to teach ways of making others do things they don't want to do. The test of success with truth talk is not that other people do what you ask, but that you ask honestly, lovingly and directly. The proof of success is when the Heavenly Father says "Well done!" to you.

We fail to receive what He has for us because we fail to ask. The same is true of our human relationships. We frequently are robbed of richness and closeness because we do not ask. Often people have been taught not to ask, for fear that others are obligated to perform whatever is requested. This is not so. Others omit asking because of a mistaken but long-held belief that asking is selfish and wrong. Many grow up in homes where no one asks directly, and consequently they have poor models from whom to learn. Passive-aggressive tactics are sometimes employed to get others to become aware of your needs, but they come from anger and cause anxiety and resentment, poisoning relationships. We learned how to make requests and how to introduce the habit of direct asking into daily speech.

FOR REVIEW, PRAYER AND DISCUSSION

1. Make up a plausible dialogue between a husband and wife, with each using nothing but questions. What's wrong with this?
2. List several ways in which people communicate indirectly.
3. Give some reasons why people resist learning to express their wants directly to others.
4. What is often the relationship between temper tantrums and failure to make direct requests?
5. Show why requests don't "force" others to comply.
6. Show why requests are not in themselves selfish.
7. Give examples showing that Jesus expressed His wants and needs directly.
8. Give five or six examples of people trying to communicate without making direct requests.
9. What do James and Paul in the New Testament write about the importance of asking?
10. What are passive-aggressive tactics? Give some examples.
11. Give some examples of hinting.
12. What is the spontaneity misbelief?
13. Repeat the most common phrases used in making direct requests.

CHAPTER SIX

Free to Say No

Has something like this ever happened at your front door?

Salesman: I want to ask you a few questions. Do you ever peel and cut vegetables?

You: (Warily) Yes.

Salesman: Then you know how odious it can be, especially with an ordinary kitchen knife. How often do you serve vegetables you prepare yourself? Once a day, at least, I'll bet.

You: Every night—almost—unless we have something like spaghetti.

Salesman: If you're using a knife now I can show you how you can make one very easy change and save enormous amounts of time and money. Are you interested in saving money and time?

You: Well, of course, but—

Salesman: Yes, isn't everybody? If you'll just let me step into your kitchen, I can show you some things that will astound you.

You: Well, all right, come on in.

The salesman demonstrates his gadget and you are impressed.

Salesman: You really can't afford not to own one. Tell you what I'll do: I'll let you have a Vegowhiz for 30% off the regular price—today only, of course. And you can't buy these in any store. It's a great opportunity. I'll just write it all up and show you what it comes to.

Let's see, here. Twelve ninety-five. And if you'll give
me your check right now I'll leave you two extra
blades.

You: Well, I don't know . . .

Salesman: Your time is worth money! Just think how much
you are going to save. You just can't afford to turn
this down.

You: Well, all right. Let me get my checkbook.

Did you really want the Vegowhiz? Of course not. Nor did
you want to spend your time talking to the salesman and watching his demonstration. Your marshmallow-textured sales resistance could have been due in part to your deep reluctance to
using the word "no."

Many people hate to refuse anyone requesting anything.
They have a fear of telling others no! Their "no-phobia" creates
situations in which others take advantage of them and of their
inability to refuse. Salesmen have a heyday with them. Unscrupulous doctors may perform unneeded surgeries. Politicians have their votes just for the asking. Clerks can make them
buy two bottles of aspirin instead of one, merely by asking,
"Two bottles or three?" Wives, husbands, children, friends, and
relatives find it easy to manipulate them.

As a result, these "no-phobics" feel abused and frequently
bewildered at just how they managed to get themselves into
the binds they are in. They get into those binds by agreeing to
what someone else has pushed on them, and then wishing, too
late, they hadn't been so quick to assent.

CREATIVE EXCUSES

The most creative activity "no-phobics" engage in is inventing excuses. When they can't think of an excuse, they're
stuck. Take Jerry, for example. As Jerry left the house he told
his wife, "I'm going to a meeting at the church. I don't know
exactly what it's for, but Jason invited me and I couldn't think
of an excuse—so I had to agree to go." Instead of refusing the
other person's request point blank, people like Jerry do their
best to fabricate or latch on to one or more seemingly solid

barriers to their fulfilling the unwanted proposal. Phrases such as "I can't because...," "We'd love to, but...," and "I would, except that..." act as little fences, protecting them from having to issue outright refusals.

Sometimes an excuse can backfire, as in Wanda's situation. Her Aunt Marge asked Wanda to let her visit sometime during August.

"I could visit you for a week or so any time during that month," she assured Wanda.

Wanda didn't mind her aunt's visits, though they did tend to prolong themselves. But Wanda knew her husband Drew would be miserable. So she searched her mind for an excuse.

"We're going camping some time during August and I'm not sure exactly when," Wanda replied with relief. "It depends on when Drew can get off."

"Oh, that's all right," answered Aunt Marge, undaunted. "I'll just keep August open and as soon as you find out when you'll be home, let me know, and I'll just pop in for a nice visit."

"That will be fine, Aunt Marge," said Wanda, trying not to show the helpless anger she felt. Wanda felt powerless. Aunt Marge would visit, despite the fact that her visit was inconvenient for Drew and Wanda. And, it seemed, there was absolutely nothing Wanda could do to control her own schedule.

This episode exemplifies one of the problems created by trying to substitute excuse-making for no-saying. Often, very often, excuses don't work. Persistent people will take another's excuses and work around them. Of course, there are times when a person can't think of an excuse. Since he doesn't want to lie, and his imagination isn't running in high gear, he is stuck. From his vantage point, he can't do a thing about it. Frustration and resentment, all carefully hidden from the other person, taint and damage what might have been a positive, love-filled relationship.

Are you the sort of "no-phobic" who simply must have an excuse, any excuse, if you don't want to grant someone else's request? Do you believe it inexcusably selfish to refuse any request from anyone just because you don't want to grant it, even if it isn't the will of the Lord for you right now? Do you always employ one of the following phrases when you would rather not do something suggested by someone else?

- "I'd love to, but I have a headache."
- "I can't. Mike said he might come over."
- "I have some work I have to do around the house."
- "My wife wants me home."
- "We can't come. My husband doesn't like things like that."
- "I can't get a baby sitter."
- "I have to do homework."

Is it vital that a person give other people reasons why he chooses to refuse their requests? Does he owe others an explanation? No!

An excellent example of this truth is the story told by Jesus of the laborers in the vineyard. The owner of the vineyard paid those who had worked only the last hour of the day the same amount as those who had harvested grapes for almost twelve hours. When the day-long workers complained he replied, "Am I not allowed to do what I choose with what belongs to me?" (Matt. 20:15, RSV). He didn't feel compelled to offer them reasons, to explain and excuse himself. And that, on a divine level, was the point Jesus was making in this parable!

If you have been brought up to believe you *must* make an excuse, that you *owe* others a list of reasons for every choice you make, particularly when you refuse a request, look again at Jesus' words. You are entitled to do what you choose with what belongs to you, so long as your choice is prompted by God's Spirit at work in your spirit. The grape grower in Jesus' parable offered no reasons for his peculiar decision except "I choose." Neither are you obligated to offer other people reasons (or excuses) when you choose to deny their requests.

Of course, you may *want* another person to know the reasons that prompted your decision. If you do, you may give those reasons. But no law of God or man requires you to do so. Instead, you may simply say things such as those below. (If you read over this list and feel butterflies in your stomach as you imagine yourself saying such things, you probably are "no-phobic.")

- "No, that won't work out for me. I'm sorry."
- "I won't be coming to that meeting. Thank you for asking me, though."
- "I don't want to do that. Sorry. Perhaps another time."

- "I won't be over next weekend. Please ask me again, will you? I really do want to come."
- "It's not a good time for you to visit. Let me get back to you when it will work out better for us."
- "I don't want to lend out my rototiller. Sorry."
- "I don't want to give to that particular cause. Sorry."
- "I really don't care to go to that restaurant. Could we choose another one?"
- "I can see you are in a difficult bind, but it won't work out for me to baby-sit for you."

WHY WE AVOID SAYING "NO"

Why do people fear and avoid refusing others' requests? I have asked many of my patients why they fear refusing others. Here are some of their answers:

"The other person might feel hurt."
"I might never be asked again."
"She might not like me."
"I might lose his love."
"I might make them angry by not going along with them."
"I feel obligated."
"I feel that I should consent."
"I know I'll feel guilty if I refuse."
"I just have the feeling that I ought to do what they ask."

These notions and feelings are so pervasive, a best-selling book, published in 1975, still attracts readers who identify with its title, *When I Say No, I Feel Guilty.*[1]

The habit of saying yes by compulsion is usually formed early. From the punitive or shaming reactions of parents or authority figures the child quickly learns that no is often, if not always, a "no-no" and that the best way to get along is to agree, whether you want to or not. Adolescents fear ostracism for saying no to their peers, and as a result many do what they don't

---

[1]Smith, Manuel J., Ph.D., *When I Say No, I Feel Guilty.* New York, Bantam Books, 1975.

really want to do, going along with the crowd to disobey God, parents, and teachers.

The habit of agreeing, of going along with whatever others ask or demand, becomes an iron cage for many. They hate to disappoint others, or see others as authorities to whom they dare not risk saying no. They believe the opposite of Romans 13:8 ("Owe no man any thing, but to love one another"). Their version reads, "You owe everyone who makes a request, because you are under the law and obligated never to refuse anyone anything." This was Vernon's problem. "I feel like such a wimp," Vernon said, wincing as he finally brought himself to get the words out. "I'm nothing but a yes-man. Gene, a guy who works with me, has me wrapped around his finger. I choke up with tension whenever I see him coming."

"Wrapped around his finger?" I asked, prying for an example.

"Yeah—like at the soda machine. He hits me for quarters just about every day. He must owe me fifty bucks by now just for the change I've loaned him."

"You give the money to him?"

"Sure. What else can I do? He follows me when I go to the machine during break. And he always pats his pockets, snaps his fingers, and says he happens to have no change right now and would I lend him a couple of quarters. I give it to him, he thanks me, and tells me he'll pay me back tomorrow. But he hasn't paid me a penny yet. Meanwhile, I'm mad enough to hit him. But mostly I'm mad at me. Why do I let myself get taken like that?"

Vernon had to be convinced it is not always and everywhere wicked to refuse anybody requesting anything. He learned he had a duty to discern and discriminate between those requests God wanted him to fulfill and those not in harmony with God's desires for him and other people. In the instance of Gene, Vernon came to see that God did not want him to encourage and foster Gene's indiscriminate borrowing, in part because it strengthened Gene's sinful disregard for the property of others.

Vernon learned to say no to Gene and to experience his freedom to refuse others in various situations.

"No, Gene," Vernon said next morning at the soda machine.

"I won't be lending you the money for your soda today because you haven't repaid the money I've already loaned you. I'm not going to keep buying your soda for you, and I'd like you to stop asking me for loans."

This wasn't easy to do, and Gene didn't like it very well. But Vernon certainly felt better. His gloom lifted, his depression cleared, and as the knot in his stomach gradually unwound, he began to feel like a person with some backbone.

THE CONSEQUENCES OF NEVER REFUSING

You may be one of those whose pain results from never refusing anyone anything. If you are, it will take special courage for you to recognize it, and take steps to learn to say no. Since refusing is frightening for you, you will try every method to avoid facing the fact that there is no other way than to go through the hard discipline of learning to turn others down.

Do you find, on examination, that your life is burdened with one or more of the following kinds of unwanted situations?

- Engaging in activities you know, in your heart, to be contrary to God's will for you, but feeling you can't control your life.
- Putting up with long and inconvenient visits from friends and relatives.
- Paying for work on your car that you didn't order.
- Talking to salesmen when you really don't want to.
- Spending hours on the phone with people you can't get away from.
- Buying things you can't use.
- Doing favors against your conscience (e.g., "I know you won't mind buying this appliance for me on your employee's discount. Nobody will ever know.")
- Going to bed with people you're not married to because they insist, though you know it's wrong.
- Accepting invitations you'd like to refuse.
- Making up "reasons" for avoiding any of the above because you don't have any other way to get yourself free.

Then you're feeling irritated, frustrated, and guilty much

of the time. Irritated and frustrated because you have lost control of your life (and you aren't giving it to the Lord, either!). Guilty because you are putting up a false front or making phony excuses which are not speaking the truth in love. No wonder you feel as Vernon did—like a wimp! Or a marshmallow! Or a wet noodle! Or a nonentity! You have worked yourself into a pattern of living in which you are always saying to yourself, "You don't count, what you want doesn't matter, you have nothing to say about anything, and your goals, desires, wishes, and preferences aren't worth any more than you are." No wonder you feel as if you have a "poor self-image"! You are dealing it out to yourself.

THE EXAMPLE OF JESUS

Did Jesus invariably say yes to whatever was asked of Him? You might get that impression from certain paintings which depict our Lord as a soft, sweet, effeminate type who wouldn't ever disappoint anyone no matter what He wanted. As Dorothy Sayers put it, they have "pared the claws of the Lion of Judah." But you won't find that sort of Jesus in the Bible. Consider the following sample dialogue (recorded in Luke 12:13, 14, RSV).

Man in crowd: Teacher, bid my brother divide the inheritance with me.
Jesus: Man, who made me a judge or divider over you?

That is a point blank refusal. And Jesus didn't offer a list of excuses either. He said, in effect, "I won't do it because that's not what I'm here for."

When Peter asked Jesus to stop talking about suffering and dying, Jesus did not say, "Oh, poor Peter. He doesn't understand but his intentions are good. So I'll humor him and go along with him." Instead, He replied, "Get behind me, Satan! For you are not on the side of God, but of men" (Mark 8:33, RSV). When God has set a person on a path toward a particular goal, indiscriminate willingness to be drawn into the plans and designs of others is "not on the side of God, but of men."

Jesus, "leaving you an example, that you should follow in his steps," (1 Pet. 2:21, RSV) was certainly the Lamb of God who laid down His life in humble self-sacrifice for sinners. But He was no weak namby-pamby, no pussy cat, no milquetoast, no spineless jellyfish who lacked the backbone to refuse requests.

Certainly Jesus taught us to say yes to the needy. But He didn't mean for us to go along with everyone about everything as a kind of automatic reflex. We are not to give in just because we haven't learned how to do anything else!

Jesus' ability to say no implies He was very familiar with Proverbs 1. A portion of that chapter enlarges on how the fear of the Lord is the beginning of wisdom. According to this section (vv. 7–19), a very important part of wisdom is knowing when not to consent to the blandishments of others. The notion that a true Christian will never refuse anyone anything is certainly clobbered in these powerful verses!

HOW TO REFUSE TO BE MANIPULATED

We shall call them Jack and Jill. They were a couple who had particular difficulty making and refusing requests. Both of them, in fact, made their requests very indirectly and manipulatively. And both had difficulty refusing without either getting angry or communicating so obliquely that the refusal wasn't clearly understood and accepted. They reported the following dialogue in one of their treatment sessions.

Jill wanted to join a health spa so she could work out with her friends, and firm up and improve her figure. She needed Jack's approval, however, because they would have to take funds from some other budget item to pay her fee. Jack did not want to spend the money. Here is how they handled the problem:

Jill: Honey, I've been thinking. You need some exercise.
(Do I need to point out to you how very manipulative this opening sentence is? Instead of truthfully stating her own request, Jill tries to make Jack want a spa membership for himself, pretending to show concern for him.)

Jack: Huh? What's this all about? I get lots of exercise cutting this two acre lawn every Saturday!

Jill: But don't you think you need to exercise more often?

Three times a week, they say, is a minimum. Besides, I
need some exercise too. So why can't we join the new
health spa?

Jack: Oh, so that's it. You want to spend some more money. Do
you think I'm made of money? I get plenty of exercise
trying to earn money faster than you can spend it!
(Jack now recognizes Jill's manipulation. But his refusal
is equally indirect and manipulative. He aims at Jill's
potential for guilt feelings. The idea is to make her feel
awful for so abusing her hardworking husband.)

Jill: All you ever care about is money. You never listen to me.
You tell me we don't have the money for anything I want
and then you go spend $8,000 we don't have for a boat!
What about me? Don't I ever get anything? All I'm asking for is a membership at the health spa so I can work
out with my friends, and you're too selfish to even listen.
(Jill, too, is an expert at guilt manipulation. She, in effect, accuses her husband of selfish, grasping greed evi-
denced by his unenthusiastic response to her wish to join
the spa.)

Jack: I'm going out! (Slams door as he leaves.)

We worked on changing the way both of them approached
the matter. Jill's request was to be truthful and straightforward. Jack was to refuse with a clear statement of his own
wishes in the matter. In this instance, because he wanted a
close relationship with Jill, he was encouraged to give her reasons for his decision. Here is the way Jack and Jill learned to
work it out.

Jill: Honey, I really want to join the health spa they're building in town. Some of my friends are going to start working out there three times a week, and I'd like to join
them. Firm up some of the flab, you know.

Jack: Want to get the old bod in shape, huh?
(Notice Jack has learned to take time to listen and to
grasp exactly what Jill wants.)

Jill: Yes, I do. And I've been looking for something I can do
with friends. What I'd like you to do is help me figure
out how we can budget the membership fee.

Jack: You'd like a little socializing along with your workout and you want us to see if we can work it into our budget. (Instead of rushing into a refusal, Jack takes pains to let Jill know he is attentive to what she wants and why she wants it. It is possible, too, that Jill will find a way to finance her membership without serious damage to the budget.)

Jill: I'd really appreciate that. When would be a good time for you?

Jack: Could you get the figures together by tomorrow night? Maybe you could come up with some suggestion about how we could afford it. I might join myself if we can work it out.

(Notice Jack's effort to be open to Jill's request rather than to close the issue without hearing her out completely.)

Jill: Sure, Jack. I'll see what I can come up with by tomorrow night.

The next night, after looking at the figures Jill has assembled, Jack finds he doesn't want to spend the $180 membership fee.

Jack: I can see that joining the spa is really important to you. But I don't like the idea of taking the money out of our savings or out of our tithe. You haven't been able to find any other allocation to cut it from, have you?

Jill: Well, no, but we could always increase our savings later.

Jack: That's true, we could. (Agreeing with what is true in Jill's assertion.) But I really don't want to do that. I feel insecure when we start using money we've budgeted for current expenses. So I'm afraid your plan won't work out from my point of view. I just don't want to do it now. How about trying to work it into next year's budget? I've got a raise coming in January, you know.

(Notice that Jack's refusal, when it comes, is clear, straightforward, and truthful. Jack takes the responsibility for it by saying twice, "I don't want to." Many people evade responsibility at this point by ascribing their choice to circumstances, talking as if their decision is forced upon them: "So, you see, there just isn't enough money for you to join the spa." Jack doesn't do that. And you shouldn't either.)

Jill: Well, I'm disappointed. You know how I hate to wait. But I guess I can hold off for a while. I want the things we spend money for to be agreed on by both of us.

Refusal in an intimate relationship such as that between husband and wife will involve many more self-revealing statements than refusal in a relationship which is not particularly close such as Jerry's in the next example.

Remember Jerry who thought he had to go to a church meeting to which Jason had invited him because he "couldn't think of an excuse"? Jerry eventually learned how to be comfortable saying no without giving reasons or making excuses. Watch him in action below.

Jason: Jerry, what have you got on for Wednesday night?
(You may recognize the manipulative tactic. Jason tries to get Jerry to tell him that the evening is free before he makes his proposal because he believes it will be harder for Jerry to turn him down once he has admitted he has no plans.)

Jerry: What's on your mind, Jason? Do you have something to suggest?

Jason: You don't have any particular committee assignments up at church, do you, Jerry?
(Jason, an old hand at manipulation, now hopes for an admission that Jerry isn't *quite* doing his duty at church. Not holding any assignments at present, Jerry certainly can't turn this one down.)

Jerry: Sounds as if you have something in mind. Tell me about it.
(For the second time, Jerry has asked Jason to make a direct request. Meanwhile he refuses the manipulative bait dangled by his friend.)

Jason: There's a meeting of the new financial planning committee up at church on Wednesday night, and I was thinking it would be a good experience for you to come and see how you like it. Maybe you might be available to be on the committee in the future.

Jerry: I won't be available, Jason, and I don't want to serve on a committee right now. Sorry. Thanks for asking me. I do appreciate being considered.

Jason: It really doesn't take that much time. We meet only one evening a month, and you wouldn't have to do anything except attend the meetings—

Jerry: Even though it wouldn't take a lot of time and I would only have to attend meetings, I don't want to do it right now. Thanks, Jason. And have a good meeting!

Jason: Well, you sound as though you mean it. Maybe some other time. Thanks anyway, Jerry.

Jerry is no longer a victim of manipulation. He has learned to say no!

Connie had a desperate case of "no-phobia." The first time I saw her she told me she had been gang-raped by four young men. As we talked it became evident that Connie had known all of them. This twenty-one-year-old woman had had sex by consent with each one of them at various times. When they discovered their "common bond" with Connie, they decided to rape her. Connie's already low evaluation of herself had now sunk to zero. Connie was convinced she was utterly worthless. Almost panicky with her need to have her value affirmed by some man's love, she was distraught because of the inattention of Gil, her current boyfriend. It seemed to her to be a dismal repetition of her previous dating relationships. She believed she would never be able to hold on to a man.

Connie: Gil hasn't called me for a week. I got tired of waiting so I called him and went over to his house. His folks were gone. He wanted to have sex, so we went to bed together. Then he told me I had to get out because his folks were coming home. I think he was lying. I don't think he wants to see me as much anymore.

Backus: What do you think is wrong?

Connie: I don't know. It happens every time. They start out and can't get enough of me. Just when I think something good is going to come of it, they begin to take me for granted. It's like as soon as sex is over they want to get rid of me or something.

Backus: What would happen if you didn't have sex with them?
Connie: Didn't have sex? I always go to bed with them. It's like I have to or they'll lose interest. I don't seem to be able to have a guy any other way.
Backus: Do you *want* to have sex with your dates, Connie?
Connie: No, I hate it. I feel guilty too. I'm a Christian and I know it's wrong. But, like I say, the guys all expect it. It's just part of the package.
Backus: Have you ever tested your theory that you have to give in to pressure in order to hang on to a man? Have you ever refused and stuck to it to see what would happen?
Connie: I've never been able to. I always panic and give in.
Backus: Would you be willing to give it a try, just to see what will happen? You know, it's pretty nearly impossible to build a close, long-term relationship around sex alone. God meant sexual unity to be a vital part of a combination of security, commitment, love, and closeness that can occur only in a permanent, exclusive man-woman relationship—that's marriage. To try to make a relationship with sex coming first is almost to guarantee failure.
Connie: I know it's not right to have sex before marriage. And I can see I'm not any closer to having a good relationship with a man. But I just don't seem to know how to say no. I've tried, but I never succeed.

I taught Connie how to handle sexual manipulation with refusal. She was a good student and soon had the tactics down pat. She was an attractive woman and soon she came in announcing that she had been out with a man she'd met at a friend's party. Connie found Greg interesting, but she was afraid he wouldn't call her again since she'd turned down his bid for sex.

Backus: Tell me about it.
Connie: I asked him in for a cup of coffee at the end of the evening. While we were talking he put his arm around me, pulled me toward him, and put his hand on my knee. I thought, *Here it comes. I'd better speak up as I've been meaning to do.*

So I took his hand, gently but firmly, put it back on his own knee, got up and took a seat close to him but opposite him, so I could look him straight in the eye. And then I did it just the way we practiced.

I said, "Greg, I want you to know that I really like you. I had a wonderful time tonight, and I think you're really cool. But I need to tell you right now that I'm not going to bed with you. I'm a Christian, and I believe sex before marriage is wrong. I want you to know that it's not that I don't find you attractive. I do. But I'm going to try to develop a close relationship with someone based on common interests and good communication, not on sex."

He was shocked, I know. He didn't quite know what to say at first, and then he smiled and said he understood, and that at least I'd said it loud and clear. We chatted for a while, I told him again what a great evening I'd had, and he left. I'm so afraid I'll never hear from him again!

Connie did hear from Greg, the very evening after our session. He called and invited her, not to his "pad" to watch TV, but to have dinner with him. Connie was ecstatic.

Notice carefully the important steps involved in Connie's refusal.

1. She physically removed Greg's hand from her body when he began to approach physical intimacy.
2. She moved physically away, but not too far away, suggesting that she was not rejecting Greg, but only the offer of physical intimacy.
3. She looked Greg in the eye as she talked.
4. She affirmed Greg and her interest in him several times, understanding that it would be easy for Greg to feel rejected and hurt by her actions unless she did.
5. She made her refusal clear and firm.
6. She made her interest in a real relationship clear. Greg will know, not only what she doesn't want from him, but what she does want in a relationship with a man. If he, too, is interested in closeness, this will attract him. If not, he might

as well look elsewhere for someone who wants nothing but a sexual encounter.

Promiscuity, however, is not the only problem that a "no-phobic" can fall into. Anger is another possible by-product.

One of Tim's difficulties was with the management of anger. He came complaining about a lifelong tendency to procrastinate to the point where he had lost several excellent positions. Examination showed, however, that Tim often got angry and flew off the handle at others. I asked Tim to log all his angry episodes for a while.

As we together combed through his anger diary, several patterns emerged. One of them was an almost invariant pattern of agreeing to requests, even when Tim didn't want to comply. Then Tim would either fail to perform (procrastinate) or become angry, furious beyond reason, at the person he felt was controlling him by requests Tim seemed unable to refuse.

We worked on refusal, training Tim to say no when he didn't want to comply. One chronic source of irritation for Tim was the borrowing habit of his neighbor, Dave. After we had worked on it for a while, Dave came over to borrow Tim's rototiller. This machine was important to Tim. He kept it in top shape, babied it, and used it very carefully. He did not like lending it to Dave every spring, but had done so for the past two years. This time he made up his mind to refuse.

Here is the conversation as Tim reported it, a gleam of triumph in his eye:

Dave: Top o' the mornin' to ya, Timmy Boy. I came over to borrow the little ol' rototiller. Gonna get my garden in early!

Tim: I'm not going to lend out my tiller anymore, Dave. How about a cup of Melanie's excellent coffee?

Dave: Oh, sure, fine. Any cream? Thanks. What's this about not lending your tiller? I've been counting on it. And I'm all ready to till!

Tim: I'm sure you've expected to borrow it again this year, since I've always lent it to you whenever you've needed it. And I'm sure you're all ready to till this morning. But I'm not going to lend it out anymore.

Dave: But, Tim, I don't understand. I've always taken good care of it. I've never hurt it, have I? I'd be responsible for any damage that might accidentally occur.

Tim: You're right, you have taken good care of my tiller and you haven't damaged it. And I believe you'd take responsibility for any damage. But I'm not lending it to anyone anymore.

Dave: How come? What's happened? I've always appreciated how willing you were to lend your things to me. Have I done something? What in the world is going on?

Tim: I know you've appreciated being able to borrow things from me, Dave, and you haven't done a thing to hurt our relationship. It's just that I'm changing some things about me. One of the things I haven't liked about myself is that I agree to things I don't really want to do and then get irritated about it. I'm trying to stop doing that. One thing I've never really wanted to do is lend my rototiller. More coffee?

Dave: No thanks. I have to get going. I guess I can go down to the hardware store and rent a tiller. I'm not sure I understand this, but I'm glad to hear I haven't done anything to upset you. I'd better be going. I want to be sure to get a tiller.

Tim: Dave?

Dave: Yes?

Tim: Let's plan a fishing trip one of these days.

Dave: Okay, sure, Tim. See you later. Thanks for the coffee.

Pay particular attention to the way Tim dealt with Dave's repeated efforts to persuade him to change his decision. Time and time again, Tim (1) acknowledged Dave's points because they were correct and he wanted Dave to know that he had been heard; (2) repeated his decision not to lend his tiller; (3) revealed his motivation to his friend, Dave, even though it meant discussing his dislike for his own past behavior.

Should Tim have refused Dave? Some readers will feel Tim was wrong to refuse to lend his tiller. And there is a question of Christian love here. Would Christian love require a neighbor to lend something whether he wanted to or not?

Perhaps. We discussed that question after the fact because Tim raised it when reporting his success at being able to say no. We agreed that Christians ought to lend to those who are truly in need. Often, however, there is no real need. As the dialogue shows, Dave found it a convenience, but not a necessity, to borrow from his neighbor. He could afford to rent a tiller, but, he informed Tim, he had dismissed the idea in favor of regularly using Tim's machine. There surely are occasions of real need when the Christian will want to lend what he has out of love for his neighbor. We decided that this was not one of them and that Tim had discerned God's way in this particular situation.

Furthermore, Tim's negative, resentful feelings which had already created a problem, were made worse every time he allowed himself to be manipulated by Dave. The destructive influence of Tim's resentment ended when Tim learned to respond to Dave's requests according to the way he felt he needed to rather than with puppet-like compliance. From Tim's point of view their relationship improved to the point where Tim looked forward to their fishing trip.

PRACTICE REFUSING

Try your hand at refusing in the following situations. You may want to write dialogues using principles learned from examples given in this chapter. Or, you may want to role play with someone else, each of you taking turns playing the part of the requester/manipulator and the person refusing the request.

- Your mechanic has telephoned to say that your car, which you brought in for routine service, needs to have the radiator hoses and fan belts replaced. You don't want to do that now.
- You and your spouse have spent Christmas with your parents ever since you were married. Your children are just out of infancy and now you want to establish some home Christmas traditions of your own. You have prayed about it together and it seems right to turn down your mother's invitation to spend Christmas Eve and Christmas morn-

ing with your parents. What you want to do is spend Christmas Eve and Christmas morning at your own home and join your parents for dinner on Christmas Day. Your mother is on the phone inviting you to come over as usual. You want to refuse and to change things. Your mother tries to persuade you to continue to celebrate Christmas her way.

- Your friend wants you to go to the movies, but you want to stay home. You have no special reason except that you don't want to go out this evening. Try to turn your friend down without making excuses.
- Your little boy wants a cookie and you don't want him to have it now.
- Your parents have always dreamed you would be a doctor. You, however, have discovered the excitement of missionary work, and you don't want to study medicine. You are to tell them you won't be fulfilling their lifelong dreams for you.
- You and your friend, spouse, or co-worker are going out for dinner. The other person wants Chinese food. You don't want Chinese food tonight—or any other night, for that matter.

FOR REVIEW, PRAYER AND DISCUSSION

1. Give some reasons why we need to learn to refuse others at times.
2. Why is refusing difficult?
3. What are some of the misbeliefs of those who find refusing difficult?
4. Suggest some times when we should not refuse others.
5. What does Romans 13 say to those who always feel obligated to please everyone else and do what is asked?
6. Give some examples of Jesus refusing requests.
7. Make up a truthful response to someone who wants you to buy something for him using your employee discount privilege. (You are not supposed to use your discount for anyone but yourself.)

CHAPTER SEVEN

Dealing with Critical People[1]

Her psychological test scores were normal. What could she be doing in a clinic for troubled people? I always study test results carefully before my first visit with a new patient, but in a few cases the person seeking help has no clinically significant psychological problems. In the case of Jenny, the problem was a critical spouse.

"I know you could help us if only Carl would come in with me," she began, looking me straight in the eye, "but he refuses to get help. He says he has no problems, and that if there's a problem, it's me."

Jenny was an attractive, slim, neatly dressed woman whose appearance concealed her forty-four years. Her emotions were under control. She did not appear depressed or nervous, and her thought processes were intact.

"What do you want from me?" I asked her. Clearly she did not, like some less well-adjusted persons, expect that I could work some sort of marvelous change in her husband at her request.

"I was hoping you could help me learn how to handle Carl's criticisms. I don't know if it's possible, but I'm getting to the point where I have to try something new. What I've done all these years hasn't worked." Jenny smiled slightly and looked

---

[1]Much of the material in this chapter is adapted from the excellent book by Manuel Smith, *When I Say No, I Feel Guilty,* published by Bantam Books, 1975.

down at her hands, presumably recalling her futile attempts to turn off her husband's put-downs. Our session continued.

Backus: What have you tried so far, Jenny?

Jenny: Well, at first I tried to handle his critical comments by showing him how unreasonable he was acting. You know, he would criticize the food or some other thing I'd done.

Backus: For example?

Jenny: Let me see—well, for example, one of his perennial themes is the way I spend money. This has been a bone of contention for years. When I come home after doing the grocery shopping, if he's home, he will watch me put things in the refrigerator and say, "What'd you buy this for? We don't need it." I explain why I bought whatever it is and why I thought we needed it. But it doesn't help.

Backus: How do you mean that? What happens?

Jenny: Well, he almost never accepts my explanation, but instead he'll argue that we don't need whatever it is, and that I'm spending all his money and driving him to the poor house. I argue my side of it, and we end up angry at each other after nearly every trip to the store.

Backus: So defending your purchases doesn't help?

Jenny: Not a bit. It just makes matters worse. I don't know what to do. Then our prayer group started studying the role of women, and I got the idea that I would just be silent and try to submit. If Carl objected to something, I wouldn't do it. I even took things back to the store if he complained about them.

Backus: Did Carl stop criticizing then?

Jenny: No way! It just got worse. He seemed to get even more critical. He put me down for the way I drove, the way I cleaned the house, even the way I sewed buttons on his shirts. I just felt angrier and angrier until I could hardly look at Carl without screaming. I'm still struggling to keep from arguing with him, but I'm not managing very well.

Backus: What do you mean?

Jenny: I can't keep up the silent act. Every once in a while I just let loose and tell him off. Then he gets his feelings hurt and we don't speak to each other for days.

Clearly, Jenny's efforts to be gentle were producing even more distress and anger than her previous attempts to defend herself. She wondered how she could forgive her husband at whom she felt almost perpetual rage.

WHY CRITICISM HURTS

Perhaps you have your own Critical Carl or Correcting Cora. No one has escaped getting criticized altogether.

Why does it distress us so to be criticized?

Most of us have been taught to please others. Our parents, for instance, expected us to please them. And what pleasure we experienced when Mother or Father would say, "You did that so well! How pleased I am with you!" And we learned very early to experience inner pain when one or the other parent found fault: "That was naughty! You shouldn't have done it that way." Their judgments meant everything. They were so big and so "always right." The bottom seemed to drop out of our world when we failed to please them.

Many people seeking psychological healing are still allowing themselves to be wounded by the ongoing criticisms of one parent or the other. Some have dedicated their lives to the fruitless task of somehow, some time, some way pleasing that critical parent: "How can I make Daddy love me and respect me? I simply must find a way!" Many 30– and 40–year-olds are investing their lives in the project of making Mom or Dad thrilled with them. Not everyone is still trying to please Dad or Mom, but most people are nevertheless hurt and angered by criticism today because of habits and beliefs formed long ago.

Those who get hurt make themselves vulnerable to criticism by misbeliefs. They believe they absolutely must please everyone else all the time. They believe that if anyone else should become displeased with them, it would be unendurable. "I've failed—I've totally failed," they wail when others are upset with them. They hurt when they are faulted and get angry when others intimate that they aren't quite perfect.

For these reasons most people consider it crucial to defend themselves when they are criticized. *I can't let that go by,* they think. So they simply have to prove that the criticism is totally wrong, that they have been sadly misunderstood, that the response they made was correct and reasonable, that the other person is a poor judge who has no right to criticize anyway. So they argue, plead their case, or attack the critic: "I had these solid gold reasons for what I did. And anyway, who are you to say anything? Remember the time you. . . ?" They may also modify their behavior to try to please the critic and avoid criticism in the future.

The residue left after all this is anger, frustration, and strained relationships. Rarely do people handle criticism effectively.

WHO DOESN'T GET CRITICIZED?

Rarely does anyone escape criticism entirely. Inevitably everyone will occasionally be criticized. Here are some examples of common, everyday criticisms:

- "Your clothes look as if you slept in them!"
- "You haven't visited us for weeks and you never call. Your father and I worry about you. You should visit us more."
- "Are we having ham *again?* Can't you think of anything else to serve?"
- "It's good but you could have done a lot better."
- "I don't see why you can't spend less for clothes."
- "People get bored when you talk so much!"
- "It wasn't very nice of you to tell us we had to go to a motel instead of staying at your place."
- "You are a cold, distant person."
- "Your attitude isn't very good."
- "Your tie and socks don't match."
- "Whenever we want you to come over you say you're busy."
- "You're always late for everything."

THE TRUTH ABOUT CRITICISM

Most of us, reading through the above list of common criticisms, would experience an automatic impulse to launch into an elaborate defense speech. We would explain that we *have* visited, and that it hasn't been more than four or five days since we called; that we haven't had ham *that* much; that we've *tried* our best; that our clothes were *just* pressed; that many people *are* interested in what we have to say; that we thought a motel would be *more* comfortable; that we couldn't *help* being late, and so on.

We usually presuppose that the critic is wrong, that we have been terribly misunderstood, and that we will not survive another minute unless we set things right or prove the fault-finder wrong. None of those common beliefs is true. Strange as it may seem, most criticism is correct. Not always, but often. Not entirely correct, but correct in a large measure. Occasionally, of course, the critic errs totally.

But much as it may startle you to learn it, the critic is ordinarily at least 90% right. Perhaps you *are* often late, unavoidable as this may be from your point of view. Maybe you *have* excused yourself several times when your friends wanted to come and visit you. You never did win any prizes for matching colors, so it's possible that your tie and socks really *don't* go well together. If you try, you can perhaps see some truth in the criticisms leveled at you.

Not only is criticism frequently correct, it may even be good for us. I didn't say it would *feel* good. But what doesn't feel good may still *be* good. God can use criticism, even painful, unfair criticism, to call our attention to need for change. Since He is at work through Christ Jesus to separate us from our sins and make us holy, we must not overlook the means He may choose to accomplish His work in us. Sometimes the means may be painful criticism.

Perhaps God desires also to teach something to the critic, particularly if the person habitually indulges in criticizing others. God's Word has some uncomplimentary descriptions of such people. One of the more humorous passages in Scripture compares them to the annoying "drip-drip" of water through a leaky roof! God does not want us to reinforce and reward these critical souls by giving them attention and a sense of importance when they carp. That, however, is the likely effect of defending ourselves or arguing when they criticize.

HOW TO RESPOND TO CRITICISM

Look in on another session with Jenny, who decided to work for a few sessions on changing her responses to Carl's critical comments. We began like this.

Backus: Jenny, you have learned that Carl's criticisms of you aren't totally false, however much they may irritate you—right?

Jenny: I don't like it but I have to admit it's often true. Carl seems to be able to swoop down on any fault or weakness I exhibit—and they really are faults and weaknesses. And even when he criticizes my actions they're always things I've really done. He doesn't just make them up.

Backus: You've also seen that defending yourself and arguing probably reinforces Carl's critical behavior.

Jenny: Well, they certainly haven't stopped it!

Backus: Are you willing to try a very different response?

Jenny: Yes, anything. What do you have in mind?

Backus: Agree with Carl.

Jenny: Agree? With the criticisms? But why? That seems like just what Carl wants.

Backus: I don't think so. I think he wants you to argue and defend. That, at least, is what happens. And he keeps coming back for more. Let's try it out. Let's pretend you are Carl and I am Jenny. You criticize me. I'll show you what I want you to do from now on. Are you willing to see for yourself how it might go?

Jenny: Sure. But what do I do? Criticize you just as if I'm Carl?

Backus: Go ahead. You be Carl now. Try to answer me as you think he would answer you in a situation such as the one we're playing.

Jenny: OK. (Playing Carl's role) Don't tell me you spent the day doing nothing but writing letters! This living room is a mess!

Backus: (Playing Jenny) You're right, the living room *is* a mess. And I *did* spend quite a bit of time writing letters.

Jenny: (Still playing Carl) You should spend more time keeping the house neat and write your letters while we're watching TV or something.

Backus: (As Jenny) No question about it. The house could use more of my attention. And I could write letters while we're watching TV in the evening.

Jenny: (Pauses, stumped) I just don't know what Carl would say if I did that. I've never done anything but argue and defend myself before so we'd be in a royal battle by this time. He'd probably respond with something like, "Well, why don't you then?"

Backus: Then you say, "That's an idea with merit. I really will consider it." In other words, you keep right on being as agreeable as you truthfully can.

Jenny: I'll try it. I really will. I can't wait to see what will happen.

Backus: Will you please keep a diary of your interactions with Carl when he criticizes you? I want you to write out as precisely as you can what each of you says and how it turns out so we can work on refinements.

Jenny: Yes, I will. You want me to write, verbatim, what each of us says when Carl criticizes.

TRUTHFUL AGREEMENT

Before looking at Jenny's diary, please notice how truthful agreement can be employed to handle criticism. The critic, from long practice, expects a response which makes clear you have been affected emotionally by his criticism. When you defend yourself or argue, you underscore that the criticism is significant to you and that he has succeeded in getting your total attention. This provides the sort of unhealthy reassurance of his importance and significance the critic is seeking.

When you assure the critic that he is right, you signal at the same time that his criticism has not hurt or surprised you. He has not shot you down. Instead, you surprise him and give him nothing to continue arguing about. This has the effect of removing the reinforcement from willy-nilly criticism, and you can thus expect its frequency to drop.

Especially important is the truthfulness of the criticism.

You probably are concerned with telling others the truth, yet often, when criticized, you try to deny or combat the criticism, true or not. You consider it important not to let any criticism stick to your Teflon-coated self; so you deny even truthful criticisms, or, failing that, supply a supposedly good reason for acting as you did.

Now, instead of arguing, begin agreeing if the criticism is truthful. Of course, if the criticism is entirely false (and a few, a very few, are), you cannot agree with it. Nonetheless, you can find alternatives to argument. For example, if someone levels a critique containing no truth at all, you can say something like, "I can understand why you might think that is the case," or, "Yes, I know how important that is to you." You can, in other words, substitute understanding for argument.

Perhaps the criticism is only partly true. The critic, for example, says, "You are always late!" You know, for a fact, that you are often right on time, but you are also a few minutes late on many occasions. So instead of saying, "No, I'm not always late," you say might say, "It's true. I am often behind schedule, and I know it irritates you to have to wait." You thus combine partial agreement with understanding.

ADDING TO CRITICISM

If you really want to stop the critic in his tracks, *add your own self-criticism to his*, and therefore take whatever wind is left out of the critic's sails. Surprisingly, it can make you feel good about the process of criticism. But more than all that, it will cause critical people to decrease the frequency with which they criticize you and will lead to more constructive ways of dealing with disagreements.

Suppose someone finds fault with you for talking too much at a party. You can add to the criticism yourself by saying, "I did talk quite a bit, didn't I? (Agreeing.) Not only that, but I probably told everybody more than they wanted to know about cars! (Adding to criticism.)"

Imagine someone tells you the meat you are serving for dinner is overcooked. You say, "It is quite well-done, for sure. (Agreeing.) It's not very tender either. (Adding to criticism.)"

Someone tells you your lawn needs mowing. You say, "It certainly is long. (Agreeing.) And what's more, the hedge needs trimming too. (Adding to criticism.)"

Remember that adding to criticism is not for the purpose of lowering yourself, but to avoid argument and not allowing the critic the satisfaction of making you defensive. And, of course, you must never add untrue criticism. Your goal must always be truth.

ASKING FOR MORE

One other truth-seeking tactic: When you have agreed with the critic and added to the criticism, *ask for more.* Try, "Was there anything else about my behavior at the party that wasn't quite the way it ought to be?" or, "What else can you tell me about this dinner that isn't up to par?" or, "What other things should be improved in my front yard?"

You may be afraid to try all these techniques for fear you'll look more vulnerable than ever. But once you do these things you'll likely discover, as Jenny did, that you have taken the rewards out of criticizing for people who are habitually on your back with faultfinding and carping. More than that, you will discover a new freedom from the devastating effects of criticism. Knowing how to handle it, you will find yourself less fearful and defensive about the critical remarks of others.

A SPECIAL CASE

One kind of criticism deserves special treatment here. Occasionally another person will tell you of some flaw in your personality. He is generally (though not always) a well-meaning individual who is not very clear about what he means. So he phrases his critique in terms so vague you have no idea what he is talking about:

"Your attitude isn't very good."
"You seemed hostile."
"You don't have a caring spirit."
"It seems as though you want to hurt me."
"I was offended by your thoughtless remarks."

All these have in common a lack of any concrete material. Not a single actual event is cited, and there are no quotations. If you are like me, you are left guessing, puzzling, and wondering about what in the world you have done to cause that person to say such things.

But it rarely stops your reflexive defensiveness from leaping up like a startled watchdog to growl, "Well, I certainly didn't mean to offend you!" or, "I think I'm as caring as you are!" or, "You're too sensitive. You think everybody's trying to hurt you!" or, "Aw, you're always getting offended at *something*!"

Such responses are untruthful and unloving. Furthermore they are about as effective in stopping criticism as gasoline is in putting out fires. Your defensiveness only convinces the critic that he was absolutely right in his negative judgments about you. These responses give an answer before one has listened to the details of the critique! Of this penchant for quick retorts, the Word of God says, "If one gives answer before he hears, it is his folly and shame" (Prov. 18:13).

The most effective possible response to a vague, judgmental generalization is a question such as, "What is there about my behavior that makes you say my attitude isn't good?" or, "What did I actually do that seemed hostile to you?" or, "What actions of mine made you feel I don't care about you?" or, "What did I say or do that made you believe I want to hurt you?" or, "Can you tell me what I said that offended you?"

Once you have obtained a concrete response, do not argue and defend. Instead, agree as much as you can. If you've been criticized for speaking harshly, you might respond with, "I guess that does sound a little hostile, now that you say it back to me," or, "I can understand why that might sound to you as though I don't care about you," or, "I can see why that might make you think I wanted to hurt you."

Then ask for more: "Is there anything else I did that hurt you?" or, "What else did I do to make you feel uncared for?" And so forth.

After hearing all that the other person has to say, try asking him if he would like to hear how you felt at the time, how your behavior appeared to you, or what you hoped your actions would convey: "I can really understand and appreciate how my actions upset you. Would you like to hear what I was actually feeling at the time and what I was hoping my actions would mean to you?"

You can then give him your perspective. Rarely do people fail to reach a new level of understanding when personal criticisms are handled in this way.

JENNY DEALS WITH CRITICISM

Jenny's next appointment was quite eventful. She had done her homework very carefully, so her diary contained an explicit account of each interaction with Carl and his criticisms. When I asked her how the week went, her smile told me she had already put some of her learning into practice.

Especially interesting was the change in frequency of Carl's critical comments. The first day Jenny logged seven! Over the week Carl's criticisms diminished notably. On the day before our appointment, though it was a Sunday and normally a day punctuated by Carl's faultfinding, Jenny had nothing to log into her diary! Evidently, Carl had learned as fast as Jenny. I cautioned her, however, that Carl's transformation might not be permanent. Old habits tend to reassert themselves. She could expect critical comments occasionally, at least for a time. Therefore it would be vital for Jenny to practice and polish her newly-acquired skills so as to have them ready when needed.

Jenny's diary showed how successfully she had employed truthful, loving, nondefensive responses to criticism: agreeing with the criticism, adding to the criticism, and asking for more. Here are some examples from her diary.

Thursday night, when Carl tasted his coffee at dinner, the expression on his face told me what was coming. Here is our conversation as accurately as I can recall it:

Carl: What did you do to this coffee? Do you stay up nights trying to figure out how to ruin coffee? It's weak enough to die of exhaustion!

Jenny: Yes, it is weaker than we like it. [Agreeing!] Not only that, it looks pale. [Adding to the criticism.] I don't like it much either.

Carl: Uh-huh, well, I guess it isn't easy to get everything right all the time.

Jenny: Would you like me to throw this potful out and try again?

Carl: No, I guess not—unless you'd rather have some stronger coffee. I'll just put a little instant powder in mine—that oughta do it.

Saturday noon I saw an unusual bird at our feeding station outside the kitchen window. I called to Carl who was in the living room reading the paper:

Jenny: Look, honey, there's a new bird at the feeding station. I think it's a chickadee. Come and look!

Carl: What's wrong with you? That's a wren. Don't you know the first thing about birds yet? We've had that feeder for three years!

Jenny: You're right. I don't know how to identify birds. Except for blue jays and robins I'm pretty much stuck.

Carl: Maybe you'd like to use my bird book. If you want it I could bring it home. I think I have it at the office now.

Jenny: Thanks. Maybe I could use it to identify some of the birds using our feeder. That would be fun.

One of the most dreadful of all occasions is the day each month when Carl reviews our financial situation. We usually get into a hassle that can last two days. This time, it went very differently.

Carl: (Looking through the cancelled checks) What's this check to Gregory's for $139.95 about?

Jenny: You already know about that. It's for the new dress. Remember?

Carl: Oh. You didn't tell me it was going to cost a fortune. Of course, I don't think you care. You don't care how much overtime I have to put in or how hard I work, do you? You never even consider that I'd like to save up enough money to retire some day, do you?

Jenny: That's true, I don't give a great deal of thought to your retirement and the difficulty of your job.

Carl:	Well, you should think about it. I have some rights, too, you know.
Jenny:	Yes, you do have rights. And you might have a point saying that I should pay more attention to your job difficulties and plans for the future.
Carl:	If you did, you wouldn't throw money around as if it were free!
Jenny:	That's true, I wouldn't.
Carl:	Then you admit you are careless with our money!
Jenny:	You're right. I am sometimes careless with our money. I'm sometimes guilty of leaving lights on or running the car engine needlessly, too. Is there anything else you've noticed me being wasteful with?
Carl:	No, nothing else I can think of. I guess we both have our faults. I don't want you to feel too bad about the dress. After all, you do look good in it.

I couldn't believe it was my husband talking. He was almost ready to urge me to go and buy another dress! From this point on, his criticisms really tapered off.

Jenny's diary included some more interactions with Carl. She had not been assigned the duty of logging criticisms of others, but she was so interested in what was taking place that she included a few interactions with other critical persons in her life. In each case Jenny applied the techniques of *agreeing with the criticism, adding to the criticism, and asking for more.* Below is an example from these interactions.

Jenny had bought some slacks, worn them once, and found that they failed to hold their color when washed. She brought the faded slacks back to the person from whom she had bought them. The interaction went like this:

THE CRITICAL SALESPERSON

Jenny:	I'd like to have a refund for these slacks. As you can see, they faded when I washed them.
Salesperson:	Looks as if you washed them in hot water. You are supposed to wash this type of material in cold water only.

Jenny: That's true, I did wash them in hot water; and it may be true that cold water would work better. I would like to have my money refunded, however, because the slacks are useless to me. And there is no tag attached to them saying they should be washed in cold water only.

Salesperson: You can't expect to get your money back, especially when you are responsible for damaging the slacks. It seems to me you should have known that this material will not stand up to hot water. The best I can do is give you a new pair.

Jenny: You're right, I damaged the slacks by washing them in hot water when I should have used cold water. And I probably should have known that cold water is best for this type of material. But I didn't, and I would like to get my money back. I don't want clothes that need to be washed in cold water only.

Salesperson: Ma'am you're really being unreasonable. We can't give everybody who ruins a pair of slacks her money back!

Jenny: I'm sure it seems unreasonable to you, and you certainly can't give everybody a refund, but I would like my money returned. I can't use slacks that must be washed in cold water only.

Salesperson: Well, I'll have to check with my supervisor. I'll be right back.
(Talks with supervisor and returns.)
Will you please fill out this form? I'm authorized to give you a refund. But we can't do this all the time.

Jenny: You absolutely can't do this all the time. And I do appreciate your help with it. Thank you.

    Please notice how often Jenny simply repeats her request for a refund. Remember the rule: When the criticism is directed at you by someone who is trying to talk you out of a goal you know is right for you, *stick to your point.* Each new criticism is simply an opportunity to agree insofar as possible, express understanding, and reiterate your request.

STICKING TO YOUR POINT

Nancy, too, had a critical spouse. But, unlike Carl, Jon was critical mostly when Nancy had a request he didn't like to consider. So Nancy learned the tactic Jenny used with the salesperson. She learned to stick to her point, as well as to agree with the criticisms. This tactic of sticking to her original point led to some real progress in her relationship with Jon.

One day Nancy decided to try once again to convince Jon they should have a joint checking account. He had steadfastly resisted this suggestion in the past. Notice how Nancy deals with the criticisms and how she returns to her request without anger or sarcasm.

Nancy: I'd like to discuss something important with you. Is this a good time?

Jon: I guess so.

Nancy: I would like you to go to the bank with me and sign the forms for a joint checking account so I can write checks when I need to.

Jon: You know how I feel about that. I don't see why you keep bringing it up.

Nancy: Yes, I know you have some negative feelings about it, and that you can't understand why I keep bringing it up. But it is really important to me to be able to use the checkbook.

Jon: You wouldn't keep the checkbook straight. In no time our finances would be in chaos.

Nancy: You're probably right. I would forget to complete the check stubs occasionally, and our finances might be in chaos sometimes. But I still want to be able to write checks on our bank account. Will you please go to the bank with me tomorrow and work it out?

Jon: You don't need to write checks. You have all those credit cards. You're never satisfied with anything I provide for you!

Nancy: I'm sure it seems to you that with credit cards I never need to write checks, and I know you feel I'm never satisfied. But I'd like you to go to the bank with me tomorrow anyway.

Jon: You're trying to take over and run things, and if you get to write checks, it'll be even worse.

Nancy: I'm sure it seems to you that if I get to write checks I'll be running our lives, and I'm sure that worries you, but I would still like for you to see that I have a check-book of my own. Will you go with me to the bank tomorrow?

Jon: You just won't listen to anything I say, will you?

Nancy: You're right, there are times when I don't pay close attention. And I don't always agree with you. Even so, I want you to go with me tomorrow.

Jon: Well, if you insist. What else can I do?

Nancy: You've got a point. What else can you do?

Nancy and Jon did go to the bank together where they completed the forms for a joint checking account. But even more important was the increased freedom Nancy began to feel in her relationship with Jon. Both of them appreciated the new peace they began to enjoy in their life together. The negotiation you just read was a first. Never before had Nancy and Jon been able to even discuss the notion of her having checking privileges without a fight and a subsequent long period of hostility. Soon the couple learned to deal similarly with other sensitive issues.

Anyone can, as Nancy did, become adept at disarming criticism and thus avoiding hostility. Without hostility the original question can be discussed and brought to a conclusion.

FOR REVIEW, PRAYER AND DISCUSSION

1. Why does criticism usually hurt?
2. How do most people believe they should handle criticism?
3. Give some examples of everyday criticisms.
4. Is the critic usually wrong? Explain.
5. How might criticism be good for us?
6. Give examples of truthful agreement in response to criticisms you invented in answer to question #3.
7. Ask someone to criticize you, and practice handling each criticism by truthful agreement. Use Jenny as a model.
8. Give some examples of adding to criticism and of asking for more.

9. Ask someone else to criticize you and respond by agreeing, adding to criticism, and asking for more.
10. Give an example of sticking to your point when someone criticizes you to avoid dealing with a request of yours.

CHAPTER EIGHT

How Matthew 18:15 Keeps You from Blowing Up

"If your brother sins against you, go and tell him his fault, between you and him alone. If he listens to you, you have gained your brother" (Matt. 18:15, RSV).

Which of Jesus' commands is more widely disregarded than any other? (Among Christians, that is.) I mean blatantly disregarded, overlooked, and violated. Not the first commandment. Most Christians aren't regularly praying to Zeus. Hardly the fifth commandment, the one against killing. Not the one against stealing, or adultery, or bearing false witness. Many believers break them all, of course, at times. But they don't disregard them.

I don't claim to have made a scientific survey to determine the answer to my question. But I have concluded, from professional experience, that the most widely disregarded of Jesus' many instructions to His people is this: If another person does something wrong, go tell him his fault.

Instead, most people try other, less constructive remedies for a brother's trespass. Take the Rev. Yack More, for instance. When he knows somebody has done wrong, he preaches against the evil. It's easier for him than going and telling his brother— alone.

Then there's Brother Gab Fest. He raises a fuss in the congregational meeting about the dark doings in the church, all the while "not mentioning any names." But everybody knows whom he means. He sees to that.

117

Everybody knows Sister Suzy Tellall. She reads Jesus' words as if they say, "Go and tell someone else between you and her alone. And tell her not to tell anyone."

There was backbiting in the apostolic church, so it isn't a recent invention (Galatians 5:15). Maybe some of the first-generation church folks had already invented what I call "gossip through prayer": "We must pray for Brother Off-The-Track. He's really been walking in sin lately. Let me tell you what he did . . . so you can pray for him, of course." Maybe they had already begun the practice of going to church leaders with other people's sins: "I think, Pastor Sheepshearer, you would do well to talk to Minestrone. He's been keeping company with a woman from the office. His poor wife! The church ought to do something."

Maybe some of the Galatian believers handled wrongdoing by trying to forget about it. Others may have handled it by refusing to speak to the one who had caused hurt. Still others may have adopted a calculated program to get even. All these tactics pointedly ignore Jesus' directions on how to handle someone's wrong behavior.

What do you do? None of the above? Perhaps you keep your brother's offense very quiet. Maybe you tell no one and instead let it fester inside you until you can hardly look the offender in the eye. You bite your tongue, pinch your lips, and try to smile as a joyful, carefree Christian.

Some who try to stifle their feelings know it isn't working because they can feel the blood rushing to their faces when they have to be around the one who has hurt them. Others, alas, won't read this book. They are so out of touch with their own feelings, so hardened with denial of what's actually going on, so accustomed to telling themselves everything but the truth about their own feelings, they will chirp the usual spiritual-sounding platitudes and go nonchalantly on their way, acting out the anger they can't even feel.

All these behaviors directly contradict what Jesus taught: Go to the person who has done something you believe is wrong and tell him about the situation. In families this divinely ordered tactic can replace nagging with marvelous results. In friendships it can do away with "the silent treatment" and thus prevent the collapse of precious relationships. In the Body of Christ it can protect the unity and community of small groups and large congregations. Because, as Jesus taught, the objective is to "gain your brother."

HOW TO DO IT

We are going to work through specific directions about how to "go and tell" someone who has done something to hurt you. And, in addition, you will learn how to respond when another person admonishes you.

BEFORE YOU BEGIN

Settle three issues in your mind before you actually open your mouth to speak. It is most desirable, though not under your control, for the other person to have settled these three preliminary issues as well. When I begin working with two people whose relationship is in trouble, as in marital or family conflict, I will insist they each agree to these premises and commit themselves to applying them rigorously:

1. *The past is past. Forgive the other person now for all that has gone before.* Unless you do, you will be burdened by the weight of all the offenses you have stored up against him. There will be no such thing as working together to resolve the one thing your brother has done to hurt you because you will be dragging in everything you didn't like since day one of your relationship.

Couples are often in trouble because one or both persons will not release the past. Their attempts to resolve an issue then become inevitably entangled in a rehearsal of unforgiven past hurts. For example:

Wayne: Sorry I'm late, honey.
Jane: Are you?
Wayne: Of course. Don't you remember, I told you I might be late?
Jane: I should remember. You've done this to me ever since we started going together. I remember our first date.

And do you know what I remember it for? Not for the lovely time we had, because it wasn't lovely. You made me wait on the corner for you and you were an hour and a half late! Do you realize that? An hour and a half late! I was so humiliated. And you've continued to make me wait for you ever since!

Jane has treasured up the past in her mind like Fort Knox hoarding gold. She keeps it where she can tap it for immediate recall. And its presence in each argument prevents any progress she and her husband might hope to make toward solutions for their problems.

Unless you forgive the past, every effort to deal with the present will become crushed under the dead weight of the past. And once you have forgiven, it is contradictory to keep resuscitating past hurts. The past is past. Forgive it in Jesus' name and get to work on the present.

2. Both persons are equal in value and in the validity of their needs, desires, wishes, and feelings. As strange as it may seem, some of my Christian clients deny the equality of persons, confusing it with the issue of authority in the home or in other structures. Notice I am not saying you must believe all persons are equal with respect to everything. That isn't true. Some people have more physical size than others; some have more intelligence, more hair, more money, more musical talent, etc. And God has ordered that some have authority over others.

But though the policeman directing traffic has authority over me, he is not superior to me in personal worth. Though the judge has authority to sentence the criminal to a prison term, the judge's needs are not more significant than those of the criminal. The parent is equal in worth to the child; the baby in the womb of the commoner is equal in human worth to the Queen of England.

If you don't believe your needs are important, equally important with those of others, you will have no basis to "go and tell him his fault" when someone in authority harms you.

Letitia, for example, believed that, as a submissive wife, she could not speak forthrightly to her husband when he rode roughshod over her needs. Instead, she pinched her lips and kept silent, though seething inside. Over time, she found her feelings hardening, and at last, in spite of exerting all her will, she was overwhelmed by hate.

When I tried to teach this poor woman to practice Jesus' own instruction to her ("go and tell him . . ."), she informed me sadly that she could not tell her husband what to do since that would be unsubmissive.

"Letitia," I replied, "do you remember who is held up as the prime Old Testament example of a submissive wife by Peter in his first letter?"

"Sarah, of course," she responded. Letitia knew her Bible.

"Correct. And what did Sarah do after she became edgy about the possibility that Ishmael, Abraham's son by another woman, might grow up to compete for first place with Isaac, Sarah's own boy?"

Letitia couldn't recall, so I told her. "She said, in effect, 'Abraham, I want you to get Ishmael out of this house. I don't want him growing up to take over what belongs rightfully to my son, Isaac.' And Abraham, perplexed, sought the Lord. God told Abraham to do exactly as Sarah had demanded. Sarah, on this occasion, had the Word of the Lord, and it was up to her husband to carry it out. Sad, but obedient to God, and respectful of the wishes of his wife, Abraham sent Ishmael and his mother away. Was Sarah being unsubmissive? Not according to the Word of God (Gen. 21:9–14)."

If you have neglected speaking to someone over you who injures you (because you believe to do so is not properly submissive), now is the time to realize that submission and authority in a relationship do not cancel Jesus' own guidelines on how to settle differences. Even a child may, and should, learn to speak and be heard when another person, whoever that person might be, is wronging him. With regard to intrinsic worth, all are equal.

3. You must be willing to make some changes yourself. Remember, you are not going to speak to your brother to vent your wrath. You are seeking change in his behavior. You want him to start acting in a different way from the way that has hurt you. But change may not proceed only in one direction. There is a chance that your brother will want you to change something, too.

An attitude of willingness to change does not imply you will thoughtlessly agree to do whatever anyone else demands. It does imply that you are willing to change behavior that is harmful to others, and you are going to remain open to change while you speak to the other person about his fault.

WHEN TO GO AND TELL

Timing is important. For instance, you almost certainly will doom your effort to get someone to change if you broach the matter in the middle of a hot argument! But many stalwart would-be admonishers sit on their peeves until a devastating argument occurs. Then, when they are "good and mad," they let the other person have it. This is not the scene Jesus envisioned when He instructed believers to tell the other person his fault. If what the other person has done makes you angry, cool off before you try to deal with his sin.

It's amazing how poor some peoples' sense of timing is. Some parents will come storming out of a child's room, yelling all the way downstairs, and interrupt what the child is doing with, "Go straighten up that room! It's terrible!" They then wonder why that child is resentful. When a person is raging mad he is unlikely to elicit anything from the other person except anger in return.

If you want to work out something with another person, cool off first and then ask for a convenient time to talk: "There's something I want to talk with you about. Would this be a good time? No? Okay, what about later this evening? You'll be free after supper? Great. Let's talk then."

DON'T

- Try to "tell him his fault" while your brother is watching the Superbowl on TV or playing "Moonlight Sonata" on the piano.
- Bring up something you consider a sin against you just as she is falling asleep in bed at night.
- Seek to practice Matthew 18:15 when either of you is

yelling, snarling, or growling. "The anger of man does not work the righteousness of God" (James 1:20, RSV).

DO

- Respect the other person's needs, desires, and ongoing activities.
- Make sure that you and the other person are both in a reasonably calm and controlled frame of mind when you "go and tell."

HOW TO TELL

"I've already told him how I feel. He knows what I don't like." This is the most common response of people to whom I suggest a program of learning to deal directly with another person's hurtful behavior. Often, they believe they have already carried out the command to "go and tell" or that it really doesn't need to be done because the other person "knows he's wrong" or "knows how I feel."

After that response I usually ask them for an example of what they have said to tell the other person his fault. And most often what they have done is wrong. Below are some examples of the prevailing behaviors my clients have imagined to be adequate, of ways many people have of "admonishing" others. Remember, all these people really thought they had done it correctly!

- "Don't you think it's about time you started getting up without having to be called?" (A question instead of a statement. Note, too, the implied exasperation.)
- "Why don't you ever think of someone besides yourself? You need to realize how hard I work around here. You ought to at least rake a few leaves this afternoon instead of making me do everything." (A question again. And the attempt to motivate with guilt. Pay attention to the "ought to.")
- "How many times do I have to tell you to pick up after yourself? You think I'm your slave, don't you?" (Implied exasperation, questions, and again, deep, dark guilt.)

- "Wouldn't you like to get the garage all cleaned up today?" (A question and the ever-popular, "Wouldn't you like to. . . ?")
- "Wouldn't you rather answer your own phone calls?" Another question. (It's just like playing *Trivial Pursuit* when trying to relate to these people.)
- "Why ask me if something's wrong? You should know what you did. And you know it's wrong, too. (The old guessing game: "Squirm, you louse, until you figure out what's eating me!")

These are examples of indirect communication. Nearly all the devices for circumventing truthful speech which we discussed earlier could be cited here as examples of ineffective ways people take to deal with the faults of others.

HOW TO BEGIN

Are you avoiding dealing with the irritations and trespasses of someone because you don't know how to get started talking to him? The following example should help:

"I wanted to talk to you about something you said to me during the committee meeting. You said you doubted my sincerity. That hurt me and made me quite angry. As a result I haven't felt able to talk freely with you. I want you to stop judging me and to come and talk with me privately if something I do upsets you. Will you please do that?"

Notice the above example includes four elements:
1. The speaker tells the listener *what he has done:* "You said you doubted my sincerity."
2. He admits *how it hurt or upset him:* "That hurt me and made me quite angry."
3. He reveals *what the consequences have been:* "I haven't felt able to talk freely with you."
4. He requests *what he wants the other to do differently:* "I want you to stop judging me and to come and talk with me pri-

vately if something I do upsets you."

THE FOUR ELEMENTS IN "TELLING HIM HIS FAULT"

Tell the other person:
  (1) **What he has done**
  (2) **How it hurt or upset you**
  (3) **The consequences (if any)**
  (4) **What you want the other to change or do differently.**

Note the inclusion of these elements in the following examples of the "opener." Study them and use them for models.

- Parent to teen-age son: "I'm having some problems with your use of the car, Jerry. Last night you took it with the gas tank half full, so this morning I had to put gas in it just to get to work. Two nights ago you used about a quarter of a tank without replacing it, and again I had to get gas just to make a trip. It frustrates me to find the gas gauge low when I want to use my own car, so I would appreciate it very much if you would regularly replace whatever gas you use. Would you do that?"
- Wife to husband: "I'm bothered by the way you corrected me at the party last night. I felt put down by the abruptness of your manner. Would you please wait until we're alone when you want to correct me for something?"
- Roommate to roommate: "The dishes you leave in the sink create difficulty for me. I don't like dirty dishes lying around, but if I wash yours repeatedly I feel resentful because it's unfair. Then I become uncomfortable when we're together because of my negative feelings. I'd like to work out an agreement to work together to keep our sink free from dirty dishes. Are you willing?"
- Boss to secretary: "I didn't like the way you interrupted me in front of that customer. It irritates me to be interrupted when my mind is on making a sale, and it looks tacky when you do it. Will you kindly wait to ask me

questions until I've finished talking to customers?"
- Friend to friend: "You've been spending more time with Agnes than you ought to, Pete. I overheard you telling your wife you had to work late. Then you had dinner with Agnes. I'm grieved and concerned, and I'm afraid that your fine relationship with the Lord is going to suffer. I'm also concerned for Joan, and I'm going to speak to her if you keep this up. I want to ask you now to stop spending extra time with Agnes and keep your relationship with her 'strictly business.' "

Perhaps you're thinking, *Why do I have to do it this way? Why is it better than my old indirect method? At least I got results—sort of—sometimes.* I don't blame you for asking. It's very hard to change old habits, especially if they are occasionally effective. But there are good reasons for including all four of the elements.

The first and most important reason is that by including all of them you *tell the truth*, and the truth is a primary concern of Christians. By admonishing in this way you are open and frank about your own feelings and reasons for wanting a change. You aren't hiding yourself and the truth about yourself behind a wall of "shoulds" and "musts" and "don't you think you ought to's," because indirect communication always evades portions of the truth. Like Paul, speaking to the Corinthians, you "commend yourself" to others with ". . . genuine love, truthful speech . . ." Your "mouth is open to" others (2 Cor. 6:6, 7, 11).

The other reason is that by using these four elements, you *must be nonmanipulative*. Including them prevents you from trying to finagle somebody into doing something because you are forced to come right out and say what you don't want and what you do want. Furthermore, the four elements involve a direct request, leaving the decision right where it belongs: with the other person.

If you follow this prescription your manner will be nonhostile and nonthreatening. You therefore will be less likely to elicit a hostile, defensive, or threatening response.

DON'T GET PERSONAL

Frequently, when I am invited to assist two people in resolving their differences, I find I am listening to anything but the issues. Before very long, each of them is engaged in an all-out effort to convince me that the other is no good, the scum of the earth, worthless, ruthless, craven, thoughtless, inconsiderate, ill-mannered, unloving, and almost without a redeeming feature.

At the same time, each labors to convince me that he himself is kind, generous, practical, considerate, thoughtful, eminently rational, truly virtuous, and without significant flaw as regards the relationship.

True, I have exaggerated. Nobody comes right out and utters all the charges and epithets I have listed. But the impression each wishes to convey is clearly expressed by these lists.

People trying to resolve problems often make the fatal blunder of personalizing. That is, they develop the notion that the problem is the other *person* and not something in the other person's *behavior*. Each abandons the aim of resolving the original difficulty and sets out to prove that the other is bad. Generally, a list of the other person's past crimes is brought in as evidence:

"Our relationship has always been jeopardized by your inconsiderate and thoughtless attitude. The first time we planned to do something together, you forgot about it—so I was all dressed to go hiking and spent half my day off waiting for you! I don't know how many times you've been late for things we planned to do together. And remember the time we were going to go to a place *I* like for dinner (for a change) and you came up with your usual 'better suggestion' just at the last minute? You never ask me what I think about anything or what I want to do. You always forget to do anything I've requested of you. Why, even your family says you think of yourself first and others second. Your father told me. . . ."

The list of crimes goes on and on. It is resurrected at every fight. And its purpose is to *personalize*. That is, to show how bad the person is rather than to deal with the offending behavior of the moment.

Below are examples of personalizing, of addressing the *person* instead of the person's offending *behavior*. You may observe that much personalizing of this kind employs adverbs of over-generalization such as *always, never, ever, completely, and totally.* (In the examples I have italicized the adverbs of overgeneralization so you can't miss them.)

- "What's with you? Why on earth do you *always* act this way?"
- "Do you think I'm made of money? You *always* act as if it grows on trees."
- "You must have the IQ of a turtle to bring the car home with a dent in that spot! You *never* look where you're going!"
- "Why don't you *ever* consider anyone but yourself?"
- "Why are you *always* such a klutz?"
- "You're a pig, eating like that. Why don't you *ever* wash before dinner?"
- "You're as tight as the rest of your family. You *never* pick up the check or offer to pay for anything."

NO PUT-DOWNS

Most personalizing involves the habit of slinging put-downs at the other person when his behavior causes you difficulty. Some of you automatically react to another person's sins with an insult. The theory seems to be that if you zap your friend, wife, or child hard enough he or she will cease the offending behavior.

What usually happens, however, is that the other person is hurt or angered by your attack. Sometimes he will zap you back. And sometimes he will store up the bitterness to poison your relationship. I cannot predict how you will be made to taste the poison later on, but you will taste it. The "root of bitterness" puts out many tendrils which later "spring up and cause trouble" (Heb. 12:15, RSV).

Put-downs are usually personal, and personalizations are usually put-downs, so the verbal behavior is similar in both instances. Here are a few examples of personalizing put-downs which may be hurled at others in a misguided attempt to correct a trespass:

- "You don't have the most elementary notion of courtesy, do you?"
- "You're just like your father; he doesn't pick up after himself either."
- "John, you look like a tramp. Go clean up."
- "Motor mouth! Can't you wait until the game is over?"
- "What are you crabbing about now?"

If you are a habitual "zapper," you may find that omitting put-downs is not as much fun as including them in your conversations with others. There is a certain wicked satisfaction in verbally "creaming" the other person, especially when you are upset by his actions. Because of that, you will have to work extra hard to tell yourself the truth about personalizing and zapping—namely that, in the long run, they create trouble for the relationship *and for the zapper.* That is because God has so ordered the universe that the fruits of *zapping* come back on the *zapper's* own head.

Jesus made clear that this untruthful and unloving speech is fraught with danger to the person who indulges in it: ". . . whoever insults his brother shall be liable to the council, and whoever says, 'You fool!' shall be liable to the hell of fire" (Matt. 5:22).

If you really want to resolve the issue and "gain your brother" (have a good relationship), you must stop personalizing and using put-downs.

NO RED HERRINGS

When people begin trying to work out their problems instead of just sitting on them, they often get mired in defensive behavior. That is, they subtly and probably unintentionally nudge the discussion off the track by defending.

Defending is nearly always a red herring. "Red herring" refers to the practice of drawing a very smelly pickled and smoked fish across a trail to confuse hunting dogs. The dogs lose the true trail and begin following the strong odor of the fish. That is precisely the way defending behavior works in a problem-solving discussion. It draws the participants away from the original issue.

Study the following piece of dialogue. The woman begins by asking her husband to change something, but he replies with a defensive and somewhat attacking remark. See how the entire conversation then drifts away from her original goal.

She: I feel awfully left out because you spend so much time reading the paper and watching sports on TV. There are so many things I'd like to talk about. I'd like very much for you to set aside some time for us to talk every day. (A terrific opener—virtually flawless!)

He: Don't blame me for not talking! (Defending) You never want to talk about anything except what's wrong with *me*. (Attacking as a defense against changing.)

She: I just don't see how you can say that. The other night I tried to tell you all about my day, didn't I? I suppose you wouldn't know—you weren't listening as usual. (See how she follows the herring's trail? She has already forgotten her aim: to get him to make time for them to talk each day. She defends herself instead.)

He: I was listening! I heard you! (Defending) You're the one who doesn't listen. How many times have I asked you not to leave my underwear in the dryer? But that's where it was this morning when I was trying to get dressed for work. (Attacking for defensive purposes works well for him. She now gets pulled far away from her original aim.)

She: Well, why don't you buy some more underwear? I can't run a whole washerload for your five pairs of shorts! (Now she is into the spirit of the thing and attacks for defensive purposes. She will avoid being faulted by blaming him for his shortage of briefs.)

He: Yup, there you go. Your answer to everything is to spend money. I can't afford to buy clothes because you're always getting a new blouse or something. What was it the other day? You needed a skirt for "every day" and it cost fifty bucks. No wonder I don't have enough underwear.

She: All right. All right. I won't try to look nice for you. You don't appreciate it anyway. All you can do is criticize me, no matter what I try to do to please you.

Now the emotions will become very intense, zapping and attacking will take over, and the goal she had of increasing their communication will be totally forgotten. The couple may even wonder, later, what it was that they fought about. Notice they did *not* fight about her request. They fought in a defending-attacking-personalizing-put-down manner which effectively prevented a resolution of the original problem. No wonder these two people are utterly frustrated, blaming one another, and not seeing why.

If the woman had stuck to her point, and even used some of the principles of receiving criticism, such as agreeing with the critic, the conversation would not have turned into a nuclear showdown.

WHEN YOU ARE THE ONE BEING ADMONISHED

Some of the rules above apply to both the admonisher and the admonishee. There are some pitfalls, however, into which the person being admonished frequently falls which will, if they are pursued, ruin communication and fellowship. They can work great harm to relationships. Here are some of the important rules for the person who is approached by another believer.

1. If someone says he's hurt—he's right! Some people meet every attempt to admonish them or request change with an attack on the admonisher for being hurt or for "making a mountain out of a molehill" or for "being too sensitive." You, too, may find that when someone else tells you how you have hurt him, your instinctive reaction is to say something like this:

> "Well, heavenly days, Marigold, you shouldn't be hurt over *that*! You're just too thin-skinned. You oughta work on not getting your feelings hurt so easily. You know I'd never do anything to harm you, don't you?"

Or like this:

> "Don't you know, Athanasius, that a Christian shouldn't feel that way? Now what does Paul tell us in Philippians? Doesn't he admonish us to think only of the

positive? I'm sure if you give the matter more thought, you'll see that you're just being critical."

When you tell another person that you have been hurt by something he said, you expect to be believed because you and you alone know when you feel hurt. Therefore, when a person says he's hurt—he's right. He is the only one who really knows.

To tell him he isn't hurt, or shouldn't be hurt, or is wrong in feeling the way he does is a put-down, a red herring, and a subtle device for defending yourself. When your brother tells you that something you have done hurts him or angers him, it isn't your place to deny or attack his feelings. Just accept him as the authority on his reactions and feelings. When he tells you he's hurt, he's hurt. And that's that.

2. *Listen! And let him know you heard.* This activity of listening is so important for developing relationships which "gain the brother" that I have devoted the next chapter to the subject. Most people do not know how to listen in conversation. They may listen to others in lectures or sermons, but when they are involved in conversation, they do everything except listen to the other person. And seldom do they bother to demonstrate that they have heard what the other has had to say.

3. *Express understanding in your response.* On a rare occasion, even when you have taken the trouble to listen to the other person, you will simply not agree that he has his facts completely correct. In that case you can at least express understanding (rather than taking exception to what he has said).

Suppose your friend has made a perfect opening speech, letting you know he really didn't appreciate your talking to his date for the entire evening, causing him to feel left out. And suppose you distinctly recall talking to your own date a good deal of the time, not to his date all the time. You are tempted to say, "You're off your rocker. I didn't talk to your girl all evening."

Instead, however, you remember this chapter and decide to express understanding even though you don't fully agree with his sweeping generalization. You do agree with as much of it as you truthfully can, saying, "You know, I did talk to your girl quite a bit. And I can understand how that might make you feel a little miffed."

Sometimes you will be able to agree, at least partially, with what the other person has told you. But even when you can't, express understanding by saying something like this: "I can understand why you might think your wishes aren't important to me, especially if you believe you told me you didn't like Mexican food before I took you to Old Mexico for dinner."

Study the following examples of understanding responses to admonition. Read them aloud. Imagine yourself responding similarly to a reproof or request for change by someone close to you:

- "You're right. I did correct you at the party in front of everyone. And I can understand why you might not feel good about that."
- "You have a point, Dad. I have used the car a lot lately without filling the tank. I was going to buy you a full tank when I get my paycheck, but I can see that you don't like always having to buy gas before you can go anywhere."
- "It's true. Joan wouldn't like it if she knew how much time I'm spending talking with Agnes at the office. And I can really understand your concern as a Christian brother, too." ·
- "I can see what you mean and why you don't like being interrupted when you're watching football. I don't like being interrupted when I'm into something either. You've got a legitimate complaint."
- "Yes, it must be upsetting to have to run downstairs looking for your underwear when you're already rushing to avoid being late for work."
- "You have a right to be angry with me about that. I shouldn't have done it that way."
- "You know, what you say makes sense. Nobody likes moving a stack of dirty dishes to get a drink of water."

An expression of agreement, or at least of understanding, prevents argument. It's difficult to keep up an argument with someone who doesn't call your statements into question.

4. Express your own desires. Now, only *after* you have heard the other person, expressed understanding, and made certain you grasp his point without arguing, defending, or attacking, you should express your desires. This does not mean you can now show the other person why he is wrong and you are right. Simply express your wishes. Describe how you would like things to go.

Here are some examples which complement some of the expressions of agreement or understanding in the previous section.

- "I want to double date with you again. I won't overdo chatting with your girl the next time."
- "I'd really like to avoid taking you to restaurants you don't like. After this, will you please tell me before we go if you don't care for the kind of food I've chosen?"
- "I want to stop correcting you in front of others. Will you help by calling it to my attention if I ever do it again?"
- "After this I'll bring the car home with the gas tank at least as full as it was when I got it."
- "I'd like to get your agreement to buy three more sets of underwear. That would help me not to have to wash quite so often."

In some situations you don't want to agree to the other person's proposal, even though you can understand completely why he makes his request. This is the place to express your own wishes in the matter. Here are examples:

- "Although I can understand where you're coming from, I want to tell you how I feel. I like to talk to everyone when Liz and I are out with another couple. I want to feel free to talk to you and your date too, to some extent. Can we work out something?"
- "Mexican food is my favorite, so I'd like us to go to a Mexican restaurant occasionally. Maybe we could work out a plan so both of us would be satisfied with the restaurants we go to."
- "Dad, there are times when I need the car but don't have the cash to buy gas. Could we negotiate some way to work around that?"
- "I really don't like washing my dishes every time I eat a snack—it's too much hassle. And besides, just rinsing and

wiping them dry isn't very sanitary. I'd like to work out something with you that would be okay with both of us."

5. *Work toward compromise.* When your wishes conflict with those of the other person, the only solution which will keep your relationship close and intact is compromise. You cannot impose your way because of some superior feature in your position. If you do, you violate the rule we laid down earlier: Treat each other as equals. Compromise recognizes the equality of each participant and the fairness involved in each giving a little to arrive at a solution.

Every Christian recognizes, in principle, that pushing to get his own way is unfair and unloving. No reader of this book has missed hearing or reading 1 Corinthians 13, which declares, "Love does not insist on its own way" (1 Cor. 13:5, RSV).

But not every Christian practices what he knows in principle. For example, when Hananiah Smith gets home from the church meeting, though he knows 1 Corinthians 13 by heart, he insists on his own way. "Because," he thumps the table for emphasis, "I am the head of this house and the Lord speaks through me alone." Meanwhile his wife, Glorianna, who also knows how to turn a Bible passage to her advantage, winks slyly and proceeds to use what she calls her "feminine wiles" to make Hananiah think he is ruling the roost.

Polycarp Tharp argues that he should get his way because his position is rational, more rational than that of Ignatius Gracious who holds that his position is based on the evidence and should therefore carry the day.

Little Tiny Smith gets her way by having a tantrum until Glorianna gives in. And young Sharp Tharp cons Polycarp by making him believe that all the other kids get it so he should too. All these situations violate the principle that "love does not insist on its own way."

Love says, "I don't agree with you. My way is different from yours. But I respect you and therefore I respect your way. Let's work out something so we can stay together through this thing." Love seeks, not to dominate, but to gain the brother.

Note, however, that compromise to gain a brother must never compromise *God's* way. Issues God has settled in His Word are not up for negotiation. But most of the issues between us and others are far from being black and white, either/or, all right or all wrong situations. On these, compromise is not only possible but effective and powerful for resolving difficulties between people of good will.

CHRISTIAN CONCILIATION SERVICES

Many Christian psychologists, psychiatrists, social workers, and Christian counselors are trained to help people negotiate resolutions to difficult issues such as marital disagreements, arguments over property, and difficulties between partners, roommates, and others. Occasionally, clergymen are equipped for such work. Recently, under the auspices of the Christian Legal Society, such conciliation services have been formally organized in a number of cities. Staffed with trained volunteers, these organizations work with both parties to help resolve disagreements. One of their purposes is to make legal actions such as divorces or civil suits unnecessary. If you and another Christian are unable to work out your conflicts yourselves, do not hesitate to use one of these resources. Often, it is just what is needed to arrive at a practical, mutually agreeable compromise.

A REMINDER

Because of the crucial nature of the material in this chapter, here is a quick review of the principles discussed. First, before trying to work out a conflict with someone, you must agree to three stipulations: (1) Forgive the past and let the past remain a bygone; (2) both persons are equal in validity of their needs, wishes, wants, and feelings; (3) you are willing to make some changes yourself.

Once you have settled that matter, observe the following principles:

- Never begin in the heat of an argument.
- Tell the other person (1) what he has done, (2) how it hurts you, (3) what the consequences are, and (4) what you would like him to do differently.

- Keep it task-and-problem-oriented; don't get personal.
- No put-downs.
- No red herrings, no defensiveness, no attacking.
- The person who is hurt is right about being hurt—don't argue that he shouldn't be hurt.
- Learn to listen (more on this in the next chapter).
- Express understanding, or, if possible, agreement in your response to admonition.
- Tell your own wishes in response to admonition.
- Work together toward compromise.

FOR REVIEW, PRAYER AND DISCUSSION

1. Recall the three fundamental premises for successful admonition.
2. Now think of someone with whom you have had a disagreement, someone you would like to face with a request for changed behavior. Can you apply the three premises to this situation and agree to all of them? Especially, have you forgiven all past hurts and sins of the other? If not, go before God and forgive your brother now.
3. Why are children equal with their parents? In what sense are they equal?
4. Why is it bad policy to begin admonition when you and the other person are angry or arguing?
5. Recall the four parts which belong in an opening speech when one goes to admonish a brother.
6. Give some examples of "getting personal" which you can imagine occurring between you and another person. Then alter your example to make them issue-oriented instead of personal.
7. What is a "red herring"?
8. What is the aim toward which most of these discussions between people should strive?
9. What about love can make you carefully consider the truth in what the other person has to say as well as in your own wishes?

CHAPTER NINE

"If He Listens to You": The Loving Art of Listening

"If he listens to you, you have gained your brother" (Jesus,
Matt. 18:15, RSV).

I once attended a class in which psychologist Dr. Val Arnold
taught the importance and skills of listening. To engrave on
our minds the necessity of listening, Dr. Arnold asked the members of the large group to pair off for an experiment. One member of each pair was to describe the qualities he wanted in a
Christian friendship, while the other person was to give every
sign of not paying attention.

Dr. Arnold instructed, "Turn away from the speaker, focus
your eyes on other things, activate your body. Do everything
possible to avoid listening or giving the impression of listening."

What an experience! The talking members of the pairs said
they felt irritated and angry, even helpless and inadequate.
Some of them stopped midway through their second or third
sentence, claiming they could not keep talking to a person who
was pointedly ignoring them.

The non-listening members of the pairs said they really
didn't hear what was said, that it was nearly impossible to
listen when not facing their partner, and that the things said
to them just slipped away.

Dramatically, Dr. Arnold had taught us the integral part
listening plays in communication, as well as the importance of
using the body to demonstrate attention by such actions as

facing the speaker, making eye contact, nodding, altering facial expression appropriately, or perhaps saying "uh-huh" occasionally.

"Squarely face the other person," said Dr. Arnold. "*O*pen your body position by uncrossing legs and unfolding arms. *L*ean toward the other person. *E*ye contact should be made from time to time (not steady staring). *R*elax and be comfortable. Remember: *S-O-L-E-R*, the keys to using your body for listening."

Because of Dr. Arnold's brilliant teaching, the members of that class will remember the crucial place of listening in serious communication. Jesus taught it long ago.

THE CRUCIAL SIGNIFICANCE OF LISTENING

If any effort to improve relationships in the body by communicating is to succeed, the persons involved must *listen*. "If he *listens* to you, you have gained your brother," is how Jesus put it. If Jesus' instruction to "go and tell him his fault" is unheeded, the importance He placed on listening is equally ignored. When was the last time you heard a sermon on listening?

To communicate well you must learn the skills of listening. No matter how well you talk, without listening, your effort will be vain. You are responsible to develop *your* listening skills, not someone else's. You must make yourself the best communicator you can be.

The letter of James, especially James 3, is a treatise on communication—the best in all literature. Like Jesus, James is an ardent promoter of listening: "Let every man be quick to hear, slow to speak, slow to anger . . ."; this hearing must be "open to reason" and should eventuate in action, not argument—"be doers of the word, not hearers only" (James 1:19; 3:17; 1:22, RSV).

Some readers of this book will devour its chapters on how to speak but neglect this chapter on how to listen. People like Quintus Schmidt. Quintus believes in communication. He's always talking. He dominates relationships. He never fails to speak loudly in church meetings. He would much rather teach than be taught, preach than be preached to, and tell instead of be told. He views communication as a one-way street.

Maybe you, like Quintus, believe the essence of communication is being quick to speak. Do you get jumpy and impatient during those portions of the conversation where it's your turn to hear? Are you so anxious to be understood that you pay no attention to the even more important skill of understanding?

A PARTY WHERE NOBODY LISTENED

I once attended a party, a professional gathering, at which I spent a good deal of energy and attention observing the other guests. At the beginning of the evening there was conversation between people in pairs and little groups. One person would talk, the other would listen politely. Then, more or less in turn, another would talk while those not speaking appeared to be listening.

As the evening hours went by and the effect of alcohol on the guests (I was the only one not drinking) became more and more evident, the strangest thing happened, which only a non-drinker could observe: *Nobody was listening!*

The talkers became louder, more voluble, less inclined to pause. People soon gave up even the pretense of listening to one another. Finally, in group after group, several people were talking at once. Speakers would look around in the hope of catching the eye of someone, anyone, who might be listening. But failing that, they talked anyhow. To get attention they increased their volume, and the party became very noisy. At last, all talked. None listened. Communication no longer existed.

This is not a diatribe against alcohol, but an example, facilitated by alcohol, of what happens when communication is destroyed by not listening. After all, it isn't only at alcoholic parties that listening is impaired. Non-listening is an epidemic. When I preach in my congregation, I, like other preachers, greet people at the door after a sermon to say "good morning." Often, the exiting parishioners will comment on the sermon they believe they have heard. Frequently, however, the sermon they think they heard isn't the sermon I think I've delivered!

Many preachers are astonished when the people they've

preached to talk back on what they believe the preacher said. Often the difference between the sermon preached and the sermon heard is enormous. Instead of listening, people actually create the sermon for themselves, perhaps supplying what they want to hear in place of what is being said.

The same problem occurs in relationships, such as marriage. Here is an example: "I give her a chance to talk!" said the male half of a husband-wife team I was counseling for communication problems.

"That's true," I agreed. "You give her a chance to speak—but you don't listen."

"What's the difference?" he replied.

And with that, he hit the nail on the head for most of us: We don't know the difference between giving others a turn to talk and listening to them.

WHAT WE DO INSTEAD

What do we do when we are supposed to be listening? Frequently, our minds are busily occupied with other projects. Here are some non-listening techniques we frequently use:

Free associating. We may hear the first few sentences. Our thoughts, however, race much faster than human speech proceeds, so we begin to associate ideas in our heads with what we hear. Now our thoughts succeed one another with lightning speed. The speaker continues traveling down his verbal highway, while we, supposedly his passengers for the journey, take off on a detour.

Occasionally, realizing what we have done, we blush with embarrassment and wrench our minds back to listen a little longer. Usually, though, when the dialogue is for some reason unimportant to us or uninteresting from our point of view, our minds wander from association to association so that we are shocked by the silence when the speaker stops or pauses.

Killing time. Some of us don't even try to listen. We kill time instead. What we have to say is the only important part of the conversation for us. Nevertheless, politeness requires that we take a break once in a while and let someone else speak. We regard this as a necessary waste of time, and proceed to employ our minds at whatever we can find to think about until a moment of silence allows us to resume speaking. How can there be any real communication with such non-listeners?

Piecemeal listening. Some of us listen just to have something to react to. We hang in there with the other person just long enough to hear an idea or a word which suggests some topic on which we can discourse. We don't actually reply. We just wait breathlessly for the speaker to stop so we can utter the gem that has occurred to us. We thus don't converse; we react piecemeal to scattered portions of what is said to us.

Waiting to argue. When the dialogue is important to us, as in an argument, we are apt to tune in with a sense of frustration, showing our haste for the other to end his speaking. We impatiently shift our gaze to the corners of the room, our posture demonstrating we are ready. At the slightest opportunity, we suck in a quick breath and dive into the discussion with our side of the argument. This is not the listening which makes for communication.

Listening to judge. Many of us listen only in order to judge others. We spend our listening time thinking, *He's too lazy . . . too greedy . . . too proud . . . too hostile,* or, *She's vain . . . self-centered . . . arrogant . . . egotistical.* As judge-listeners we imagine we can discern negative motives in others, and thus supply our judgments freely. We are unable to discriminate what we actually observe with our senses from what we construct with our minds. The following situation exemplifies judgmental listening:

Scott asked Georgia to go to a party.

She replied, "Thank you so much for inviting me, Scott, but I would rather go to church that night. I find I really need that fellowship, and I end up regretting it whenever I don't get it."

Scott later reported to his roommate: "Georgia is self-righteous. What a prude! She thinks she's too good to go to a party with me and uses church for an excuse. That's hypocritical, for sure."

Scott felt rejected by Georgia (though he hadn't been rejected), and to make up for the hurt he felt she'd caused him, he constructed judgments. Had he really listened instead, he might easily have made a date with Georgia for the next evening.

A CLINICAL EXAMPLE

Mitch and Link were good friends who had formed a business partnership. Their new racket club, under construction, promised to thrive as soon as the courts opened. Lately, however, they found themselves frequently disagreeing. Mitch, for example, wanted to add another court large enough to accommodate local volleyball teams. Link was certain the extra court would never pay for itself. Here is their discussion:

Mitch: Link, that volleyball court will bring people into our place who have never played racketball. They'll see the game and want to try it. Presto! New customers!

Link: Just how many new customers is it going to bring in, Mitch? You don't have the faintest idea. Only one thing we know for certain: It's gonna cost more—a lot more. The changes we'd need to make in design will come to at least ten bucks extra per square foot. And that's not conjecture.

Mitch: I think we should take a chance. It's bound to pay off.

Link: And I think we ought to use our heads. You don't seem to appreciate that business costs are very real.

Mitch: What you really mean is that you can't stand not running the whole show. I'm a partner too, you know.

Link: You're an airhead, man, trying to play it your way even if it bankrupts us.

Mitch and Link came to the clinic to get some help with their negotiations. They were right in concluding that they didn't communicate well. What they didn't realize is that the problem they had was actually a failure to *listen* to each other.

When an argument began, each would listen only to judge the other. Notice Mitch's last speech ("You can't stand not running the whole show."), and Link's final judgmental attack ("You're an airhead . . ."). Both judged the other person's intentions and motives unfavorably. In such statements the imputed motives are always negative.

It is impossible to guess another person's inner thoughts and motivations. It is hard enough to know your own motives. The person who listens only in order to judge another cannot be walking in the truth.

WHAT HAPPENS INSIDE THE NON-LISTENER'S BRAIN?

Imagine a friend is telling you about the trouble she and her husband are having with their teen-age son. The boy has just been arrested on a robbery charge. What goes on in your head? What is your internal monologue like? Might it be something like this?

> Thank God, I'm not in her shoes. I wonder what she and her husband did to that kid. Maybe it isn't the way they raised him; maybe it's all in the genes. Wow! They have to go to court with him! The thought makes my stomach flip-flop. What would I do in their shoes? How would I feel? How does she keep smiling? Oh, I'd probably manage too. Am I glad we raised ours right. Or at least picked out the right gene pool. It really is pretty dumb of them not to see that it's good for the kid to get caught. Even if he has to go to an institution for a while, it's probably the best way.

Perhaps you let your associations run on freely while your friend is talking. You let your mind wander to related thoughts, thinking about things you have read or heard. Your own notions speed through your head.

Instead of empathetically putting yourself into your friend's situation, you may give yourself a relieved pat on the back for being clever enough not to be there too. Or you might pass judgment on your friend. Or if your friend is merely dull and boring, you might be thinking of a way to turn the conversation around so it interests you.

In any case you wonder how you can recapture the limelight. And you spend some time planning your response. What you *don't* do is listen!

THE ELEMENTS OF GOOD HEARING

"Let every man be quick to hear . . ." implies that hearing is something done with energy and effort. It isn't a process of passive absorption.

Here are the activities you must learn to perform to be a good, loving, truthful, "quick" hearer: *attending; active reason-*

ing; creative empathizing; intuiting; letting the Spirit enlighten; facilitating; and giving feedback.

Attending. To be a good listener you must learn to attend. Attending is a response. In everyday speech, the word "attend" means little more than getting your body there, as in "I attend church every Sunday, but I sleep through the service." The true meaning of the word, however, involves an action of your mind.

Most people think of listening as passive, like being a cup someone else is filling up or a recording tape on which a magnetic head is rearranging the molecules. But your mind is not a cup or a tape. It isn't a blotter, passively soaking up drops of speech. You must use your will and direct your mind to what the speaker is saying.

In order to practice attending, imagine you are taking notes while the other person speaks. Picture a tablet you are writing on. Since you can think much faster than the other person can talk, direct your mind to recall and note down on your imaginary tablet the points the speaker has been making. Lectures, sermons, and speeches are opportunities to practice active attending. Of course, this tactic is valuable in conversation as well. When you have successfully rehearsed in your mind the things the other person has been saying, reward yourself with mental praise and satisfaction.

Active reasoning. How fast can you think? Psychologists have attempted to answer that question in the laboratory. The speed of thought is much greater than that of the fastest speaker on earth. Because thoughts flash like electric currents through the mind, you can accomplish much thinking while you're listening.

To exploit your mind's capacity to think so fast, verbalize the speaker's rationale or reasoning process (not just the points he is making). Make his case for him in your mind. Rehearse his reasons for believing and saying what he is saying, as Rod is doing in the following example.

Imagine Janet is explaining her desire to take some college course at night. While she talks, Rod, who is learning how to listen, actively reasons with her, verbalizing (in his mind) her rationale, in this manner:

"She believes I am being challenged daily in my work,

while she has stagnated. She would like to feed her mind too. Besides, she seems to think I might be more interested in conversation with her if she had some college level material on her mind to talk about."

Reread Rod's thoughts and notice he follows Janet's reasoning process as closely as possible. He purposely avoids planning how he will argue with her, passing judgment on her motives or reasons, or thinking about what his answer will be. He employs all his mental faculties to enter the train of her thinking and to grasp how she is reasoning. This is probably what James means by being "open to reason" (James 3:17).

Creative empathizing. With empathy we tune into another person's feelings. We imagine what they are like. We enter creatively into the experiences of the speaker. We think, *If I were you, in your location, squeezed by the pressures now squeezing you, thinking and believing as you think and believe, reacting biochemically the way you are reacting, I would be feeling as you feel. I will make an effort to imagine what it would be like to experience your feelings.*

Sometimes when I am treating a patient, there is a moment of near-perfect empathy. The patient's woes are mine. His impaired ability to cope with life is mine. His sense of stark hopelessness is mine. The pain in his heart and tears in his eyes are mine. This is truthful listening. This is what the Bible means by "rejoice with those who rejoice, weep with those who weep" (Rom. 12:15, RSV).

Cultivate and develop the habit of empathetic listening. Learn to ask yourself, as the other person is speaking, questions such as these:

- How does he feel?
- What is he telling himself now?
- What would it be like if I were experiencing and believing the things he is experiencing and believing?
- Can I imagine coming from where he is coming from right now? Can I assume his role for a moment?

Then you will be able to give him answers, rather than just talk to him.

Intuiting. If your mind is attuned only to what the other

person is saying, or to what you are going to say when he stops talking, you may be ignoring an important element in listening: *your own feelings.* Notice how June makes this mistake in the following example.

June hardly noticed that she frequently developed a knot in her stomach when Robert was talking. She worked at listening to her husband, always attempting to fabricate a response, but totally ignored her own feelings.

At last, June visited her physician, complaining of burning sensations in the abdomen. He diagnosed an ulcer.

Had June paid more attention to what is commonly called "gut-feelings" she might have been able to sense the painful anger that accompanied her dialogues with Robert. She would have realized that her interpretations of her husband's speech "made her mad." She and Robert might then have worked out ways to resolve the problem of her aroused anger. But as long as June ignored her feelings, she was able to pay attention only to the things Robert said, and was forced to ignore her own emotions.

Intuition includes something called "recipathy." Different from sympathy and empathy, recipathy is one's own feeling, experienced in response to another person's behavior. It requires thinking, not, *How is he feeling right now?* but *How am I feeling when he is speaking?*

You may be surprised at the range of emotions others can elicit in you. Joy, yearning, sadness, love, anger, hatred, fear, anxiety, apprehension, frustration, irritation, fury, poignancy—all are possible. At various times you may have the desire to touch the other person, hold him, wipe his tears, hit him, or push him away from you. Sometimes you may want to yell at him. Pay attention to your intuitions, and to the feelings you are experiencing as a result of them.

Letting the Spirit enlighten. Christians will vary in the amount of experience they have had with this dimension. Every believer has been enlightened by the Holy Spirit. Most Christians have occasionally noticed the Spirit's communication of truth about current experiences (e.g., conviction of sin during a sermon on the subject). But not everyone, when interacting with another person, listens for the Spirit's whispers. A person can, by praying for sensitivity and practicing awareness, learn to be open to the Spirit's speaking.

Very often, while listening to a patient, I find I must rely on the voice of the Holy Spirit from within to give me understanding of what is happening. A psychologist, contrary to what many people think, cannot see through his patient. My scientific training prepares me to make inferences on the basis of your behavior, inferences which may seem miraculous. But they are not miraculous. Therefore, as I perform psychotherapy, I often need to be guided to deeper knowledge by the Holy Spirit. By the Spirit I am enabled to know some things which are not communicated through the senses. This supernaturally given material is sometimes referred to as a "word of knowledge."

In the very same way, you can pray for the enlightenment of the Holy Spirit in conversation. Sometimes the Spirit will moderate your listening and thus change the response you would have given. Here are some examples of the thoughts He might place in your mind:

"Your husband truly loves you, even though right now you are aware only of the fury you feel at him."

"Easy does it. You can blow your top now and get angry. You can tell yourself you've been provoked and you have a good blowout coming. Or you can control yourself, calm down, and suggest that both of you cool off and continue a little later when you aren't so upset. That will work out much better, you know."

"What you are believing now doesn't have to make you hopeless if you will put hope in Me. I am your Rock. What that person is saying now cannot take away the firm foothold you have when you take your stand on Me."

"The things he is saying are false. He doesn't understand his own motives and has conned himself into believing what he is telling you. But they are not so."

"Stop telling yourself misbeliefs about what you're hearing. You know very well nothing that person says can make you inferior or inadequate. So instead of singing that sad song to yourself, tell yourself the truth."

Listen to the Spirit. He will help you to tell yourself the

truth, moderate your reactions, and give you skills for loving listening.

Facilitating. Surely you have had the experience of trying to talk to someone who did everything but make the conversation easy. Remember? He didn't really look at you. His eyes kept searching the room. It seemed as though he was looking for someone else who might interest him more. He responded with the most rudimentary grunts to what you were saying. When he did say something, it was so unrelated to what you were talking about you knew he hadn't heard you.

How did you feel? Like ending the conversation as fast as you could? Like crawling in a hole? Like asking yourself what was so dull and uninteresting about you that you couldn't keep the other person's attention? For certain, you didn't enjoy the experience, did you?

Perhaps you learned something though. And it might help now if you did. You could have learned how *not* to do it if you want to be a good facilitator in communication with another. And if you didn't learn, here are tips on how to be a good facilitator:

A good facilitator turns and inclines himself toward the speaker, not rotating around the points of the compass looking for other things to do.

A good facilitator keeps eye contact. This doesn't mean he must maintain a constant, unblinking gaze at the other person. But he should look into the eyes of the speaker most of the time he is talking. He may look away occasionally, but should return his gaze to the speaker's eyes.

A good facilitator constructs comments which draw the speaker out. "Yes, I understand." "Tell me more about that." "Can you expand a little bit on how you felt?" "I would really like to hear more about your thoughts on this. Could you fill me in?" Notice how open-ended such questions and remarks are. They encourage the speaker to talk and give him the feeling that he has the listener's full attention.

Giving feedback. This is the most critical element of good communication. Feedback is vital, especially on sensitive or very important issues. Giving the other person a sense of what you have heard him say is the best way to verify what has actually been communicated.

Giving feedback means telling the other person what you have heard him say, what reasoning you have understood him to be using, what feelings you have perceived in him, and what feelings have been elicited in you. Sometimes, but not always, feedback may include what you have heard the Holy Spirit say.

It is best to intersperse feedback comments throughout the dialogue rather than make a long feedback speech at the end. Feedback is easier to give when the speaker has not gone on so long the listener's memory is unable to retain what has been said.

In giving feedback, paraphrase what the speaker has told you. Don't merely repeat back the exact words spoken to you, but try to capture the sense in your own words. Below are some examples of feedback. Study the examples and use them for practice so as to develop the skill of feedback by paraphrase. You will need to use it in the negotiation process you studied in chapter 7. The first group contains examples of feedback which conveys the speaker's thought content as heard by the listener—a simple paraphrase.

Joan and Elroy:

Joan: I would like to landscape our backyard, put some paving stones around the beds, and run a little stream through the center of the yard ending up in a pool over by the cedars. We have plenty of water in the pond, so all we would need is a pump to get the stream started.

Elroy: You'd like to do some paving in the backyard and to run a stream through it using water from the pond. Sounds good to me.

Andy and Clarice:

Andy: I know you want to get an evening job to help with our expenses, but I don't want you to. I come home at night tired. I want a good dinner ready for me, and then I want to relax rather than help with housework and put the kids to bed. I know that if you worked we would end up with more stresses than the earnings you bring home could offset.

Clarice: You feel that my getting a job wouldn't be worth the extra trouble it would make for you. Also, you don't want to come home, fix dinner, clean house, and put the kids to bed after you've worked hard all day. You'd much rather rest in the evening and have me do the household duties. You believe we'd end up with more stress and not much more money if I worked in the evenings.

Doris and Jane:

Doris: Jane, I want to talk with you about cleaning the apartment. I haven't liked your clothes lying around the living room. Also you frequently leave your popcorn popper on the table and dishes in the sink. For the last three Saturdays you've gone out, and I have mopped the floors, cleaned the bathroom, and scrubbed the kitchen sink. I want you to pick up after yourself and share the cleaning tasks on an equal basis.

Jane: I understand what you're saying. You feel it isn't fair that I haven't done any hard cleaning for the last three weeks, and you don't like my clothes and dishes left out after I'm through with them. You want to divide the cleaning chores up evenly between us.

Here are some examples of feedback conveying the speaker's feelings as discerned by the listener.

Jonathan and Miriam:

Jonathan: I don't like the idea of going to visit your parents this weekend. It's my only chance to watch football and do some things around the house, and I don't want to spend my time sitting around talking to your dad about his store.

Miriam: You're feeling aggravated about going to visit my parents for a whole weekend. Even the thought of it makes you feel frustrated and bored.

Janice to Joel:

Janice: As I was listening to you talk about your boss, I got the feeling that if I were in your shoes, telling myself what you are telling yourself, I'd have a sense of hope-lessness. Is that what you're expressing to me?

THE SATISFYING SKILL OF GIVING FEEDBACK

The skill of giving feedback is the most satisfying communications skill a person can acquire. It is satisfying to you when you are giving the feedback, because it relieves you of the responsibility of planning an answer and frees you to truly listen. When you learn to do it you acquire the habit of taking responsibility for hearing, understanding, and feeling what another person is saying and meaning. Listening in this way feels good because it is loving and respectful.

Your feedback-giving habit is also satisfying to the speaker. How many times you've experienced speaking up, only to feel ignored or unheard by the other person! When another person gives evidence that he has carefully and empathically listened, you feel harmony, peace, and trust in the relationship.

THERE IS NO SUBSTITUTE FOR FEEDBACK

A small sailing boat was disabled about seventy miles off the California coast. A storm had broken its mast and disabled its ship-to-shore radio. Now the two men aboard had only a small citizen's band radio on which to broadcast their cry for help.

Far away in Minnesota, a visiting friend turned on his hosts' CB radio out of curiosity—the startled family heard the distress call being broadcast from the Pacific! Such long-distance communication with a CB radio is an anomaly called "skip." There is no way to return such a signal. Nonetheless, the listeners could take steps to help the troubled sailors.

The Minnesotan called his local sheriff, who called the Coast Guard; the two men were rescued, and their crippled boat was towed to shore. All this took several hours.

Meanwhile, however, though the sailors had communicated their distress and position truthfully and precisely, they had no way of knowing they had been heard until they saw their rescuers approaching. Until that moment their misery was unabated because they had no idea their cry had been received by someone and help was on the way. That incident illustrates well the importance of feedback. Feedback lets the speaker know he is being heard. A good listener, therefore, is one who gives appropriate and frequent feedback.

ANALYZING YOUR LISTENING HABITS

You have just read about how to solve one of the most distressing problems in communication: not listening. Sometimes, people don't listen because they are too anxious and tense to hear well. They concentrate on their nervousness and miss what the other person has to say.

In our clinic we teach social skills to anxious people. That is, we try to train them in appropriate social behavior and speech. Usually I model a piece of verbal behavior by doing it for the client. Then the client imitates it. After I state the response, I try to get the client to do it just as I did.

Amazingly, the client rarely plays the speech back correctly. Even short responses of a few words are, at first, repeated wrong. Do you know why? It is because a client rarely hears what he is supposed to say. And that is because the thought of trying that new response arouses great anxiety.

I then try to get such a person to calm down, get his mind off his own performance fears, and work at the process of active listening and attending.

Getting anxious and nervous about what you are going to say; focusing attention on formulating your response; judging, condemning and forming negative opinions about the speaker; or simply letting your thoughts wander because you are sitting passively like a piece of blotting paper instead of listening actively—these are the major barriers to effective listening.

On the next page is a checklist you can use to improve your listening skills. You might want to memorize and keep it in your mind during conversations. Then check through the written list after any serious or important conversation you may find yourself in. Active listening is not vital in banter or small-talk, although it helps a good deal in some ordinary social talk to at least pay attention to what is being said. But active listening becomes extremely important in serious discussions between people trying to resolve difficulties and disagreements.

After each such conversation, check yourself according to this list:

_____ I actively attended to the other person by mentally repeating what he was saying.

_____ I actively verbalized in my mind the speaker's rationale and worked through his reasoning. I was able to state his case effectively to myself.

_____ I put myself in the speaker's shoes and creatively tried to feel his emotions.

_____ I paid attention to my own feelings. I exercised recipathy and made myself notice the emotions aroused in me as I listened.

_____ I tuned in to hear the Holy Spirit's voice in my heart.

_____ I used eye contact, bodily posture, and encouraging phrases to facilitate the other person's speaking.

_____ I gave the person feedback by paraphrasing what I heard, telling what I felt, and saying what I thought he felt.

FOR REVIEW, PRAYER AND DISCUSSION

1. What single skill is most critical for good communication? (Without it there is no communication at all.)
2. Give a New Testament passage which urges this skill on us.
3. Most people erroneously believe the main thing in communication is being quick to _____.
4. What are some of the things people do instead of listening while others are speaking?
5. Describe the person who listens just to have something to react to.
6. Give an example of listening to judge.
7. List seven skills which are involved in good hearing.
8. Tell how attending can change you into an active listener rather than a passive blotter.
9. What is empathy? What does it have to do with hearing?

10. What is recipathy? What does it have to do with hearing?
11. Give some examples of facilitating.
12. Make up some examples of feedback. Include some thought feedback and some feeling feedback.

CHAPTER TEN

Wrapping the Truth in Love

"Mr. Blaine, I was wondering if you would give me time off work to take that assertiveness course they're offering at the community college." Walter had finally built up the courage to make his request.

"No way!" replied Tom Blaine, owner of the auto parts store where Walter worked as a clerk. "My wife took that course, and ever since she learned all that stuff, she's been impossible to live with!"

Maybe Tom Blaine was only revealing his need to dominate others. Perhaps he was one of those who think they have a right to push other people around. It's possible that he meant only to surround himself with human doormats on whom he could wipe his feet.

Maybe not. Consider that the assertiveness class in question might have taught Mrs. Blaine little more than how to be obnoxious. Perhaps the "communication" she learned conveyed to others nothing but fleshly selfishness. She actually may have become "impossible to live with." Such programs offered by some worldly "trainers" are little more than formalized exercises in "looking out for Number One."

What's the problem? Why do training programs, meant to help people communicate, become twisted? Why are the products of these programs sometimes graduated as outspoken creeps? What's wrong when knowledge puffs up people rather than building bridges between them?

LOVE, THE MIGHTIEST POWER IN THE UNIVERSE

Again, we will look to the fourth chapter of Ephesians. Here Paul offers a wealth of Spirit-inspired guidance for communication. Thus far we have concentrated on his injunction to "speak the truth." But in verse 15 Paul adds the words "in love." If we have tried speaking the truth and it has only made others wary of us, the problem could be that we haven't made the effort to speak truth *in love*.

The greatest power in the universe and the most potent force available to man is love. Not assertiveness. Not "standing up for my rights." Not telling other people off. Not blowing up whole nations with nuclear bombs. Not scientific research. Not technology. The greatest power ever known is the power of love.

Love brought the world into being. Love moved God to send His Son to identify with the fallen race of men and yield up His life for our salvation. Love broke the stranglehold of sin, of death, and of the forces of evil.

KNOWLEDGE MAKES ARROGANT

"Knowledge makes arrogant, but love edifies" (1 Cor. 8:1, NASB). Learn all the lessons this book holds, except the lesson of love, and you will have no more than educated arrogance.

Knowledge of psychology can unlock powerful resources. Knowing all there is to know about what makes people tick can bestow awesome power over others. The ability to predict and control human behavior can mean almost unlimited possibilities for getting your will done. C. S. Lewis, in his great novel, *That Hideous Strength*, makes this point; he imaginatively portrays global disaster that results from a vast increase in scientific knowledge, unmixed with love of God or man.

Many people try to learn more about human behavior so they can effectively manipulate others. For example, when I teach social skills and communication courses, someone often engages me in a dialogue like this:

"Well, I tried what you taught me with my husband and it didn't work."

"What do you mean, 'It didn't work'?"

"He didn't do what I wanted him to."

You may be tempted to read this book as a manual on how to get your way. You may even practice its methods to get power over people. You may, unconsciously, lengthen its title to read, *Telling Each Other the Truth (So As to Make Others Shape Up According to Your Specifications)*. This is what Paul means when he writes, "Knowledge makes arrogant."

Knowledge without love leads to manipulation. Any program to acquire knowledge and skills can go sour if knowledge is amassed without love. Such loveless knowledge promotes manipulation, the underhanded control of others. Manipulation often tries to make the other person feel guilty, anxious, depressed, or helpless in order to pressure him into doing what he may not want to do. Using knowledge to exploit a person rather than caring for him comes from learning *tactics* while failing to learn *love*.

This statement is an example of loveless manipulation: "I don't understand why you never come shopping with me the way other wives shop with their husbands. I feel like you don't care even slightly about my needs."

This statement is not manipulation, but a loving, truthful request: "Will you please come with me and help me pick out a new shirt at the shopping center?"

Knowledge without love leads to dictation. I have often seen people who have learned something about the teachings of Scripture on authority in the home use their new knowledge to abuse others. They take what they have learned and put it to work for themselves, issuing orders right and left or hinting around manipulatively. They issue dictatorial statements: "Get that garbage out!" "Hurry up!" "Where's dinner? I'm the head of this house and I'm home now."

In the arrogant dictator you can see knowledge puffing up. Every word coming out of his mouth says, "I'm big stuff around here."

Knowledge without love leads to abrasive behavior. The abrasive behavior of some who have taken worldly assertiveness training courses furnishes an example of knowledge without love. Much of their speech with others is filled with selfish demands coated over with supposedly assertive phraseology: "I want you to . . . I don't like . . . I feel angry about . . . I'm not going to do that for you, and I have a right to refuse . . . I have a right to expect you to . . ."

They cease doing anything others ask them to under the rubric of their newfound "rights." They begin badgering others with their new vocabulary of wants and wishes. Nothing kind or thoughtful comes out of their mouths. They believe that by thinking of themselves first, last, and always, they are "really communicating," or "healthfully fulfilling themselves," or "creatively self-actualizing." The only connection in which they think of "love" is in juxtaposition with "self," as in "self-love."

Pleased with their newfound self-love, they may or may not notice that others avoid them. If they do, they ascribe it to the fact that their friends only want to use them anyway, so let them go. They will find new friends who are as "into" self-actualization as they themselves are.

Without love, all you have learned in this book can become hideous, self-aggrandizing knowledge. Do your words puff *you* up or build *others* up ("edify" means to build up)? Does your speech enhance your own "big stuff" image, or does it make others glow with the importance God declares they actually have? Evaluate your use of what you have learned so far to determine whether it puffs you up or builds you and others up, and study to make your speech not only true, but loving.

LOVE BUILDS UP

Unfortunately, few words are more bandied about than "love." It often means anything the speaker wants it to mean— and therefore it means almost nothing.

The following is a list of ideas the word "love" is apt to evoke in our culture. A quick reading will demonstrate why it might be hard for us to think concretely about the love that builds up:

> Love may make you think of romance, feelings, friendship, attraction, sexual acts, heart palpitations, warmth, closeness, perversions, pining in sadness, affairs, high emotional arousal, desire, enjoyment, affection, savoring, benevolence, harmony, fondness, beauty, pleasantness, passion, ardor, adoration, tenderness, idolization, regard, popularity, charity, lust, fervor, admiration, fancying, yearning, libido, infatuation, ecstasy, rapture, enchantment, spiritual coupling, flirtation, hanky-panky, self-sacrifice, service.

So what does "love" really mean? When the writers of Scripture mention love, it may occasionally carry some of the meanings in the box above, for the Bible recognizes the full range of human feelings. Uniquely, however, the biblical authors speak of a love unlike the usual human emotions. Most often, their use of "love" has no relation to vague feelings, friendship, or attraction. Instead, the Scriptures tell us we are to love especially those who fail to attract us—our enemies. Therefore, the word must mean something besides positive feelings about other people. And it does.

Love means acting in the other person's best interests. If I love you, I speak the truth to you, not only for my benefit, but for yours. I seek the best not only for myself or for those to whom I feel drawn and attracted, but for all those with whom I associate. In all my actions, including my speech, I am to work for the other person's highest good.

But doesn't love mean I have to do what the other person wants, regardless of my feelings or desires? Doesn't love mean I give up my own judgments, thoughts, feelings, and wishes, and simply perform whatever another person requests of me? Not at all! Such "love" might even serve evil purposes, since it would make me an obedient servant of the other person's whims, whether good, bad, or indifferent. Such "love" might conceivably turn the other person into a whining, demanding, spoiled brat, as in the case of ill-informed parents trying to give their child misconceived "love" which grants all wishes. He becomes a monstrous little creature, intolerable to others, impossible with peers, and dominated by the misbelief that the universe exists to cater to him.

Obviously, I do not advocate saying and doing whatever the other person thinks is in his best interest. Loving another means discerning, saying, and doing what *really* is in his best interest.

Don't, therefore, in the guise of loving others, simply say what sounds good to them. Rather, speak the truth that *is* good for them. Don't merely bandy pleasantries and spray compliments around, but consider what is both true and good before you speak. Not merely, "What would Merilee like to hear me say?" but, "What is true and good for Merilee to hear?"

This kind of love requires sacrifice—you may, after all, risk your friendship by telling the other person the truth *in love.* But the love that ultimately lays down life for the other person is the love you want to incorporate into your truthful communication.

CHARACTERISTICS OF LOVING SPEECH

Since this is a book about speech, we will concentrate our attention on loving *speech,* rather than on the entire spectrum of loving behavior. First Corinthians 13 details a number of characteristics of the love we're discussing. These qualities mark all loving behavior, but are wholly applicable to the matter of loving speech. The rest of this chapter details principles drawn from this passage of scripture.

Loving speech doesn't put down. Instead of put-downs, loving speech will contain positive, rewarding phrases and words. Paul writes that love is "kind," that "it does not rejoice in wrong." Name-calling, put-downs, and zaps, on the other hand, are attempts to hurt others, or to revel in wrong, in another's sin. Pay attention to that unloving quality as you read the following examples:

"You stupid idiot! How could you be so dumb?" (Here the rejoicing is in the pain inflicted on the other person.)

"The only reason you brought me these flowers is to get your way again, isn't it?" (Here the other's motive is judged and put down.)

"Well, Genius, why all the C's on this report card? Teacher persecuting you again?" (Sarcasm is rarely loving. Rather, it is painful humbling of the victim.)

"Wait till I tell you what I heard up at church! Is it juicy!" (Gossip uses the misfortune and misbehaviors of others for one's own aggrandizement.)

"Hey, everybody, Sam's just asked a girl to go out with him—and, guess what! She told him to go jump in the lake!" (In front of Sam, giving occasion for Sam to make himself feel mortified and develop further his belief that he is worthless and unloved.)

Loving speech rewards others. "Love . . . rejoices in the right." It will make positive statements, reinforcing the good in others. The psychological law of reinforcement assures that whenever an action is followed by a positive event, the person is more likely to do that action again. If you, for instance, told me that this book was helpful to you, I would be more likely to write another book, since your statement was pleasant and rewarding for me.

Think how often you miss opportunities to put this principle to work. Instead of clobbering other people with zaps and attacks, gossip and put-downs, you could reward their positive behavior with love in your language. You could practice love talk instead of guilt talk, instead of hurtful talk, instead of sarcastic talk, instead of threatening talk, instead of condemning talk, instead of insulting, humbling, punishing, demeaning talk.

When your spouse does something to please you, don't take it for granted; show your love by saying something rewarding. When your child tries hard to achieve something, but fails, show your love by saying something rewarding; don't merely find fault and punish. Positive speech, not threats and criticism, undergirds good discipline.

The components of love talk, of rewarding speech, include: praise, thanks, smiles, bragging about the other person—rehearsing in front of others the good things he has done. Love talk will often include nonverbal expressions such as hugging, kissing, patting, squeezing, giving attention and showing interest in the other, doing things for the other, cookies, candies, flowers, money, favors.

But whatever you do, *don't hide hornets in your reinforcers!* My youngest daughter, Debbie, was chilly, so she went to her closet and wriggled into her warm exercise suit. Thirty seconds later her left hip felt as if it were on fire. A hornet had hidden in a fold of the suit, so instead of snug warmth, Debbie had put on a sizzling, white-hot jab in the hip. A source of comfort had become a source of agony.

The same can happen in speech if love is tainted. In the process of giving a reward, of saying something loving and positive, many people think, *But the act I'm rewarding wasn't quite perfect, and I wouldn't want to reward the imperfect part, so I'd better include a qualifier.* The result is the hornet in the reinforcer. The person receiving it feels at first as though he is being loved and ends up feeling the jab of the stinger. Some people are so accustomed to including zaps in their reinforcers that they almost never truly reinforce anyone.

Here the zapper tries to reinforce her little girl who has just dried the dishes for the first time in her young life: "Thank you for doing the dishes, Emily. That was so nice of you. And they are lovely. But look at the water marks you left on the glasses. You must do better next time, darling."

What little Emily gets out of this is a painful message: You didn't do a good job. If the zapper zaps routinely, this little girl will likely grow up with a full set of perfectionist misbeliefs, constantly bugging her with the notion that nothing she does is really good enough.

Some people seem always to include the hornet with their reinforcers:

"It was nice of you to think about cooking dinner, but you forgot I don't like garlic on my meat."

"That was a fine sermon, but I don't agree with your interpretation of the passage you used for a text."

"Thanks for taking me to lunch. But I shouldn't have wasted so much time with you."

"You played a great game, except for the fly ball you missed in the third inning."

Notice the following examples of rewarding, loving speech—no hornets. See if you don't feel better as you read them than you did reading the zapping "reinforcers" above.

"I really appreciate you."

"I love you."

"I like you."

"I care about our relationship, and that's why I want to work this out with you."

"I really enjoy being with you."

"What can I do for you to show you I appreciate you?"

"You were great tonight."

"You did a marvelous job."

"Wow! Wearing this shirt you gave me made me a celebrity! I was the center of attention all day at work. Everybody stopped to admire it."

"Thank you for what you did for me."

"Thank you for washing and ironing my clothes."

"Thank you for working so hard to support all of us."

"You are wonderful! I'm so pleased you thought of me and invited me."

"You paid a lot of attention to me at the party. I really appreciate that!"

A note of caution: Beware of the perverse habit of bestowing reinforcers on others when the relationship is in trouble.

Ronson, for example, told me with great self-satisfaction that he had given his wife, Lena, some flowers: "They did the trick, too," he crowed.

"Just what 'trick' were they supposed to do, Ronson?" I asked, pretty sure I already knew.

"Well, we got ourselves into a hassle and Lena wouldn't talk to me. It went on for hours. And, believe me, it can actually continue for days at our house. But this time, I said to myself, 'I'm going to put a stop to it right now.' And I went right out, bought a dozen roses, handed them to Lena, and she put her arms around me. Something pretty great happened next. Flowers'll do it every time!"

I said, "Not such a hot idea, in my opinion!"

"Worked better than some of your ideas," Ronson replied, miffed. "What's wrong with it, I'd like to know."

"Nothing, if you're trying to train Lena to pout and frown silently whenever she's upset with your behavior. Is that what you want to do?"

"Huh? Of course not. I want her to discuss her problem so we can work it out."

"You must remember, Ronson, that whatever behavior you reward is the behavior most likely to occur every time similar circumstances arise. If you give Lena flowers when she pouts, she will develop the pouting habit into a real art."

Ronson, like many other people, feels strongly that no one should be rewarded for doing good—they're only behaving as he expects they should. So, unfortunately, he waits until others behave in ways that hurt him. Then he gives them the attention and love they would like to get from him when they do well.

Are you one of those who fawns over others when they cause you trouble and ignores those who are supportive, loving, and helpful to you? Like Ronson, you are probably rewarding behavior which is the opposite of what you would like others to be and do.

If you don't learn another thing from this chapter, learn to bring home flowers, fix special meals, bestow extra attentiveness, and offer positive reactions to others *when they have done things you like and appreciate*, and *not* when they are angry or giving opposition.

Loving speech admits faults. "Love does not insist on its own way." Open to criticism, willing to listen, and willing to admit faults, loving speech does not engage in defending and attacking. (See chapter 3.) Loving speech is not defensive or aggressive, even under provocation.

Here are some examples of loving speech, paired with their defensive counterparts. Wouldn't you rather learn love talk?

Loving Speech	*Unloving Speech*
Have I done something to hurt you?	What's the matter with you? Can't you ever be happy?

I see I've upset you. I think I've said something that hurt. I'm sorry.

What have I said this time? Are you ever sensitive!

You've made me see I've hurt you. Is there any way I can make up for my stupidity?

Now I've done it again. Whatever I try to do, you aren't able to accept it without getting your feelings hurt. Would it help if I stood on my head?

You're right. It wasn't very kind of me to do all the talking and exclude you.

I didn't do *all* the talking. Besides, you never say anything anyway.

You have a point. And now that you mention it, I agree that I could have been more thoughtful than I was.

I'm as thoughtful as you. What about the time you forgot even to visit me in the hospital?

You've got a point. I should do a better job of taking care of our lawn than I do.

I do as good a job as any other guy in the neighborhood!

You know, I haven't paid as much attention as I could to dressing neatly. Thanks for calling to my attention the mismatch between my shirt and tie.

I'll dress the way I want to. You wouldn't know when things match and when they don't anyhow.

As you say, it was careless of me to overlook putting gas in the car.

I'm always putting gas in your car. Once in a while I'd like to use some of it.

LOVING SPEECH AVOIDS ANGER.

Love "is not easily provoked." To be hard to provoke means to be irenic, seeking solutions and compromises. In his own eyes a great hero, in God's eyes an unloving bully, the man who never seeks compromise, but makes each of his wishes a matter of principle on which he firmly plants his big unmoving feet, is not speaking truth in love. Love attempts to avoid anger and conflict.[1]

---

[1] You can learn more about avoiding anger from the book *Telling Yourself the Truth* by William Backus and Marie Chapian. Here you can observe that dealing with anger requires that you learn to speak to others in truth and

"I care. Let's work it out. I don't want to give up on our relationship. I'd like to find a way for the two of us to solve this." That's a free sample of peacemaking speech. It makes a great substitute for: "Drop dead! I don't care if I never see you again. So there."

You will find that peaceful speech is nearly impossible unless you have first, quietly, under the impulse and direction of the Holy Spirit, talked to yourself in a manner like this: "Now, cool it, Ginny. He's just pushing your buttons. You can keep yourself from getting angry, and you'll be able to handle this just fine if you do. Try a soft answer."

Practice controlling your own self-talk when you feel that someone else is getting under your skin.

LOVE IS LONG-SUFFERING

You have finished reading this book. You have practiced hard, kept logs, and changed your speech. You now know how to request change, and you are very effective at it. You have done all you can. You have offered to change yourself. You have spoken positive, reinforcing truths.

Question: Now what if the other person continues the same old patterns of undesirable, offensive, unwanted behavior? He won't change, no matter how hard you try. What then?

Answer: Put up with it.

The biblical bottom line is this: live through it. If nothing you say to the troublemaker helps, no matter how scientifically and psychologically potent it is, no matter how grounded in the Word and truth of God it may be, then God's Word to you is "Hang in there."

If you live with a husband who is difficult, a wife who's impossible, parents who are utterly beyond belief, or children who remain incorrigible, *put up* with them. If you face a roommate who won't negotiate, a pastor who won't minister to you, a boss who makes irrational demands, associates who violate

---

love, as well as that you learn to change how you speak to yourself. Further discussion of the art of managing anger is offered in *Telling the Truth to Troubled People* by William Backus. Both of these books are published by Bethany House Publishers.

your expectations right and left, *put up with them*—for as long as the Lord leaves them in your life. Love is long-suffering.

One of our most dogged misbeliefs is the notion that we should not have to put up with any fault or failing in anyone else. We should be expected to relate only to perfect people. We should live in a universe where others always treat us fairly, squarely, nicely, positively, and lovingly. And if, perchance, we come across someone violating our norms, it is our right to get upset, to scream and yell, to end the relationship, to stage a protest, to walk away with our marbles and refuse to continue the game. We have, most of us, grown up believing it is awful if someone does not treat us precisely the way we want to be treated.

The truth you must tell yourself to learn long-suffering is this: *God has not given me a contract guaranteeing I will always be surrounded by people who do nothing but right, good, true, and fair things.* God has never promised a universe where the behavior of other people will be sinless toward you. When you stop being shocked at the sinful behavior of other people, you will find your angry outrage replaced by patient long-suffering.

Maybe you have been telling yourself, "How outrageous that he should treat me this way. I never would treat him so. I shouldn't have to take this. It's just terrible that I'm being subjected to it. Furthermore, I can't stand it any longer. I have every right to yell and object and get myself good and angry—maybe even do something drastic!"

Try this instead: "I have no reason to expect that so-and-so will be perfect. I don't like his behavior, and I don't have to like it. I don't approve of what he is doing, and I don't have to approve of it. But I have known since I was a tot in Sunday school that human beings sin. So I am neither surprised nor outraged that I haven't been able to make so-and-so change in the way I want him to. I am disappointed, especially since I worked so hard at it, but I can handle it. I don't have to upset myself. I can keep my cool, and I can go about my life without relying on him to change right now. Perhaps at some other time the change I want will occur. Meanwhile I can pray for him, love, and reward him for any small positive actions I like and appreciate. I can hang in there and keep myself in control."

WHEN LOVE MUST INFLICT PAIN

Sometimes love inflicts pain. God is pure love, yet He willed the suffering of Jesus, His only-begotten Son! Even when Jesus pleaded, "Father, if thou be willing, remove this cup from me," the Father, strong in love, ordered His Son to drink.

I love my children. Yet I deliberately inflicted pain on all of them at various times. Spanking three-year-old Christa when she went into the street was an act of love. Temporarily depriving sixteen-year-old Annie of the use of the car when she drove dangerously was an act of love. Martin and Debbie too could tell you of similar acts of love which, when they occurred, seemed painful.

At age ten, Christa grasped this principle so well she decorated a special stick, lettered it with the label, "The Rod of God," and contributed it for loving application by her parents!

Rarely does the world understand the sort of love which loves enough to hurt, to deny requests, and to minister frustrations and corrections. But such love is the love of God and of the people of God.

Sometimes it is necessary to address someone with truthful speech which hurts. A loving parent may have to say truthful words to a child though the child would rather not hear them: "I haven't liked your behavior this afternoon, especially when you yelled at me in the store. So I'm not going to give you a cookie."

A spouse speaking the truth in love may have some things to say which the other spouse finds painful: "I didn't like the way you talked to David today; it seemed flirtatious to me."

The point is that we cannot measure love solely by whether or not what we say hurts someone's feelings. The fact that another person may not like what we have spoken does not automatically mean we have done wrong.

Nellie, for instance, was nearly at her wits' end. She did not want to go out with Glen. But Glen kept asking her despite her excuses. One time she told him, "I can't go to the movies with you because I have to study." Another time, "I have to visit my sick aunt in the hospital." At other times, "I'm too tired." "I may be out of town." "I have to wash my hair." "I think I'm having company that night." Nellie tried all the time-worn, barely truthful excuses she could think of, but Glen kept calling.

"Why don't you tell him you don't want to go out with him and you would like him not to call you?" I asked her. "Wouldn't that be the precise truth, Nellie?"

"Sure, but that would hurt his feelings!" she responded, her tone implying that I had suggested something akin to assassinating Glen.

"Probably it would hurt Glen some. But what do you think you're doing now? Your thin excuses are telling Glen not only that you don't want to see him, but also that you don't think enough of him to level with him about it. Talking straight to Glen might hurt at first, but not as much as any other alternative you can think of."

"I guess you're right. Stringing Glen along isn't loving him. I think I'm probably just trying to make it easy for myself. And what I'm doing isn't easy after all. I'm beginning to feel like a creep. I think I'll tell Glen not to call anymore. It'll be hard, but it's the best way in the long run."

Nellie finally told Glen straight-out that she didn't want to date him. Glen's reaction surprised her. He thanked her for her openness, and suggested she keep her options open and give him a call if she ever did feel like seeing him again. Then Glen offered to have coffee with Nellie and to share openly with her how he had felt while she was putting him off with her excuses.

Eventually Nellie became curious. She called Glen and they did get together for coffee. After a little small talk, Glen explained his reaction to Nellie's excuse-making tactics.

"It wasn't easy," he confided. "I knew you intended to put me off, especially after the second or third call. But I wasn't completely certain of your reason. You might have been just shy—or you could have had some other reason for turning me down that you didn't want to tell me. Of course, I realized the most likely explanation was that you didn't want to see me. It's always been hard for me to risk any kind of rejection, but I was so strongly attracted to you I decided to force myself to keep calling until you either dated me or told me truthfully you didn't want to." Glen was open and straightforward as he divulged all this to Nellie.

Nellie began to realize there was a lot to this young man, and that her first impressions had been based on superficial evidence. She offered to see Glen again if he still wanted to get together. The last time I saw her, Nellie was dating Glen exclusively and they were beginning to wonder whether the Lord had perhaps meant them for one another.

This example of Nellie and Glen is probably more typical than it appears to you if you are unaccustomed to straightforward speech. It offers a graphic illustration of the truth that loving speech may, in the long run, mean choosing to say what hurts rather than what seems easy. And it certainly illustrates the benefits of truthful, loving speech!

THE SOURCE OF LOVE IN YOUR SPEECH

The well out of which the water of love must be drawn is the love that glues the universe together: the love of God. Infinite and incomprehensible, all-embracing and self-giving beyond any human model, God's love sets a pattern for us to follow which both encourages and discourages. God's love encourages us because the Creator and Father of us all commands us to do nothing He has not already done himself. It can discourage us, too, because we can never achieve the perfection and oceanic depth of His love. By the Spirit's power we can imitate but we cannot duplicate His love.

In fact, those who do not truly know God cannot even begin to love with His love. That is because they stand outside the realm in which they could experience His love. God loves them but they haven't yet recognized or become aware of that love.

There is, according to Jesus, one way to the Father and His love. That is Jesus Christ himself (John 14:6). If you have not yet traveled that way, you can do so right now. You can turn from your sin, your disobedience. You can believe that He died for your sins and because of that, your Father forgives them all and receives you fully into the circle of fellowship with himself and all the children of God who really experience His love in Jesus.

You can say, right now, in your internal monologue (or self-talk), "Lord Jesus, You are *my* Savior from sin and death, my

Savior from deceit and lovelessness, too. I believe this and I thank you for this gift. I choose to follow your example of love by the power of the Holy Spirit whom you send into my heart now as your Gift of Life. Amen."

Now comes into your psyche the divine power without which none of the love of God could direct your own behavior and speech, the power of the Holy Spirit dwelling within you. Now you can love with the love of God, as well as be loved by the love of God.

FOR REVIEW, PRAYER AND DISCUSSION

1. What is the sorry result of some worldly training programs in "assertiveness"?
2. What is the mightiest power on earth? Give some reasons for your answer.
3. What, according to 1 Corinthians 8:1, may be the result of truth (knowledge) without love?
4. What temptation could beset people who are working through this book without giving careful attention to the goal of this teaching?
5. What can knowledge without love lead to in relationships?
6. Give some examples illustrating your answer to question 5.
7. How can the concept of "rights" be misused?
8. Give a few of the multitude of ideas evoked in our culture by the word "love."
9. In Scripture usage, the word love most often means _____ _____.
10. Why is it important not to interpret the word "love" as meaning "Give the other person whatever he wants"?
11. Give some examples of speech which "rejoices at wrong."
12. Love in our language should ordinarily be rewarding to other people. What kind of things do we often do instead?
13. What is the mainstay of good discipline?
14. What are "hornets in your reinforcers"?
15. Give some examples of reinforcing speech.
16. Loving speech admits _____.
17. Give some examples of your answer to #16.

18. Loving speech is not easily _____.
19. Give some examples of peaceful speech.
20. Tell about some self-instruction you will need to give your-self to control anger and exhibit peaceful speech.
21. What does "long-suffering" mean in plain English?
22. Give some examples of loving speech which might inflict pain and still be loving.
23. Where must you begin if you wish to learn to love others?

CHAPTER ELEVEN

Telling the Truth in Social Talk—Small Talk

Helen was seeking psychological help, but not for the usual reasons. She was not suffering great anguish. She was not plagued by jumpy, anxious feelings. She was not ridden with unwanted habits too tenacious to break. In fact, Helen was considered a success by all who knew her. Excellent progress in her graduate studies at a prestigious university portended a bright employment future. She wasn't beautiful, but she wasn't ugly or repulsive either. All-in-all, things looked good for Helen.

Except for one thing. Helen had no friends. She had relatives back home and acquaintances on campus, but not a soul she could properly call a friend.

Here is an excerpt from our first conversation:

Backus: What do you mean by a "friend"?

Helen: Someone I can talk to and be close to. I don't feel free to phone anybody just to talk. And there's nobody I can open up to.

Backus: Do you have any theories about why?

Helen: No, I don't. I try to be pleasant to people. I greet them and observe all the amenities. I don't get it.

Backus: Do you join organizations, go to parties, work at meeting people and chatting with them?

Helen: I hate those things. Sitting around, trying to think of something significant to say, having to listen to chit-chat turns me off!

Backus: What is there about socializing that bothers you?
Helen: Well, I can never think of anything to say. And I don't think people are interested anyway. I know I'm not enthralled with what others are saying. It all seems to be "much ado about nothing."
Backus: You don't like small talk?
Helen: I certainly don't. And I see no sense in it.

Is it difficult for you to socialize? Do you find it unpleasant and uninteresting to engage in what is often called "chit-chat"? We will refer to this sort of speech as "small talk" because it is talk about small matters, generally indulged in with no great sense of gravity or importance.

Anyone may have trouble with small talk. He may be the brilliant intellectual who cannot let go of his heavy thoughts and just chat about anything and everything. Or perhaps he is the hard-driving type "A" business person whose one-track mind breaks its restless mulling over job-related matters only to grab a few hours' sleep. Again, he might be the shy, anxious, jumpy type who glues himself timidly to the wall in the darkest corner he can find when other people gather for social talk.

Such people usually have one thing in common: they have never learned to indulge in casual conversation. They haven't acquired the skills of small talk.

Chattering, getting acquainted, socializing, shooting the breeze—did Jesus occasionally "let down" and participate in purely social conversation? Some people think not. They can't envision Jesus smiling or playing. They never let themselves imagine He could have engaged in the random palaver of ordinary human beings at social gatherings.

The Bible certainly cautions us against indulging in coarse joking and foolish chatter with immoral content (Ephesians 5:4 condemns such vain speech). But I find nothing in Scripture that forbids moderate social discourse. Nowhere does it say, specifically, whether Jesus and the apostles practiced small talk or not. We can only conjecture.

In my opinion, they did. We know they observed other social amenities appropriate to their culture, and occasionally this would include attending a party or a dinner. They went fishing or hiking when they needed a break. More than likely their camaraderie included more than just formal teaching and learning. The picture I have of their mealtimes, for instance, is not that of a monastic refectory where all remain silent at the table while one reads from an appointed text. Rather, I envision men and women in relaxed desultory conversation, recounting their experiences, expressing their feelings, likes, and dislikes, and discussing together the events of their day.

Perhaps some of those who cannot imagine Jesus indulging in companionable small talk are unable to get the hang of it themselves. A common deficit among workaholics, introverts, and blue-nosed legalists suspicious of any pleasure, the inability to make small talk can be remedied by those willing to work at it. Those who are very shy, to the point where they become tongue-tied in nearly any social situation, especially where interaction is with more than one person at a time, will need to practice the skills offered in this chapter.

Some people, however, though not particularly shy, have obtained what reinforcing attention they get from others by speaking of deep, serious subjects. Consequently, they attempt to retain a little place in the limelight by uttering weighty speech on every occasion. Like people who are inhibited by shyness, these heavies feel lost in sociable contexts where the conversation is light and given to rambling. Preachers, professors, doctors, psychologists, and business people often remain nose-to-the-grindstone types because they are lost for something light to say in a circle of chatting acquaintances.

"WHATEVER IT TAKES, I DON'T HAVE IT"

"But I can never think of anything to say," Helen told me when we got to the subject of hobnobbing with others.

"It's not easy for you to participate in group verbal behavior?" I suggested.

"Oh, I'm fine when I'm giving a report to the class or discussing an assignment with someone. But where I have trouble is in social groups. I walk up to people standing together in the halls and feel like a fifth wheel."

"Like a fifth wheel?" I wanted her to go on.

"Yes, 'I don't belong here,' I keep telling myself. They are

talking about football and I don't know a thing about football—
or, for that matter, any other sport. And when they discuss
politics, religion, or horseback riding, it's just as bad. What I
know somehow doesn't seem to fit in, so I don't come up with
anything to toss into the conversation pot."

"Do you ever try to chime in?"

"Not very often. When I do, nobody pays much attention. I
might ask a question and not even get an answer, it's that bad.
Whatever it takes, I don't seem to have it."

Helen's case is not unusual. The experiences of varied types
of people deficient in the skills appropriate to small talk are
very similar. Note these statements that crop up frequently in
counseling sessions:

- "No one talks to me."
- "I can never think of anything to talk about."
- "People don't notice me at all."
- "I feel out of place."
- "I try to say something, but nobody responds."
- "They're always talking about subjects on which I'm un-
  informed."
- "I tried to break in by asking a question, but nobody an-
  swered it. It was as if I wasn't even there."

DOES SMALL TALK SERVE A GOOD PURPOSE?

Very frequently, such people exhibit a defensive disdain (or
even raise "spiritual" objections) to small talk. "I can't see any
purpose in it," they complain. "It's just a waste of time."

You have, perhaps, consoled yourself for your deficiencies
by telling yourself that whatever it is you can't do very well
isn't important anyhow. You may have handled your awkward-
ness with social talk by doing some of the same things Helen
did.

When I suggested she learn sociable chatting, Helen objected: "It's boring, and I never enjoy it. Why learn it? Besides,
I can't see that it serves any purpose. It seems to me people
would be better off if they talked about serious matters. There
are so many problems in the world, so many significant issues

in human life, so many burning spiritual topics, I don't see why I should waste time and energy on chewing the fat!"

Are you puzzled about the purpose of what you might call "idle chatter"? Do you, like Helen, mildly resent that you are, evidently, expected by others to engage in light, insignificant banter about nothing in particular when your head is full of serious issues? Or are you, perhaps, anxious and tense at the very thought of participating freely in the recreational conversation of a group? "Why should I make myself so nervous?" you want to know.

"Helen," I suggested, "social conversation does serve some purposes. Let's take a look at some of them."

"Go on." Helen was not one to waste time.

"Well, to begin with, what may look like aimless chatter provides a setting for two people to meet each other and perhaps begin a friendship."

"But couldn't people get to know each other just as well if they discussed the theory of electromagnetism or something else *interesting*?" Helen was becoming impatient with me.

"Not very likely, Helen. In fact, your suggestion illustrates my point. How many people are you likely to meet in a social setting who are proficient in your technical, scholarly pursuits? As a matter of fact, one of the primary purposes of small talk is to give people a chance to know a little about each other and about each other's interests and experiences. After the discovery of mutual interests, conversation can pursue a path both people find exciting. Or else—and this is equally valuable— two people can discover they have few common interests and move on to get acquainted with others."

"I see," said Helen. "In other words, small talk conveys some important information, tiny bits at a time, so people don't come on to each other all at once." Helen was getting into the spirit of the thing so she continued. "I remember meeting a guy at a party once who told me in the first sentence or two of our brief conversation some intimate details about his personal life. It was too much for me to handle, all of a sudden, and I remember feeling it was inappropriate for him to reveal so much so soon."

Helen's rather exceptional experience made a point perfectly. Namely, that small talk enables people to get acquainted a little at a time. Total openness and intimate self-revelation from someone one has just met creates problems very difficult for most people to handle.

Here is a summary of the purposes of small talk as I outlined them for Helen: Small talk enables people to (1) start relationships and, in some cases, begin to build friendships; (2) get to know and be known a little at a time, meanwhile testing the waters of a new acquaintanceship; (3) pass the time pleasantly and entertainingly.

HOW TO SMALL TALK

Make your questions interesting. Most people think they would be wisest to ask questions of the other person when they find themselves in the untested waters of a new acquaintanceship. For example: "What did you think of tonight's speaker?" "How do you think the election's going to come out?" "Where are you from?" "How long have you been a member here?" "Have you known the Smiths for some time?" These all might be openers for a small talk conversation with one person. In a pinch.

Questions, however, can be dull and prosaic. If they are the same old questions everyone asks, social conversation can develop the automatic, monotonous sameness Helen complained about.

I tried to show Helen, however, that even questions can be made interesting. I suggested, "Helen, see if you can improve on some of the more routine, get-acquainted questions by asking them in ways that provoke thought." She was equal to the task.

Instead of "What did you think of tonight's speaker?" as an opener, Helen came up with, "Tell me what, for you, was the most important point tonight's speaker was making?"

Instead of, "How did you like your visit to Israel?" she suggested, "What did you find on your trip to Israel that would especially interest me? What should I make a point of trying to see or do?"

Rather than, "How long have you been a member here?" Helen thought more interest might be sparked by a question such as "What about this organization made you want to join it?"

Spend some time thinking about how you can improve your small talk questions to elicit interest and responsive enthusiasm from other people. Practice inventing questions you believe will make the other person think.

A note of caution: Don't fire questions one after the other as if you were holding an interrogation or conducting an employment interview. Remember to intersperse your questions with statements offering your own point of view, background, interests, and feelings. And give the other person a chance to initiate topics or ask questions too.

Learn to tell stories. Spend some time listening to the social chit-chat of others, carefully noting the tactics of those who skillfully gain attention in a group. If you do this you will probably discover that the best social talkers are those who tell stories well.

Questions are not enough. If you try to break into a group with a question, you may discover that no one responds. Or the response will be perfunctory and you will be as lost as before. What you must learn to do is tell stories. Experiences. Your own or those of someone else. Perhaps something you have read or heard in the media. Occasionally a joke.

The person who avoids small talk with a shudder has very likely never learned to narrate. If you have a problem with social talk, get-acquainted talk, hob-nobbing-with-new-people talk, the chances are excellent that you haven't mastered the art of telling stories.

Jesus was a master storyteller. He rarely talked without stories. He must have learned to file away the things He saw and experienced in such a way that He could recall and share them with others. After all, it need not matter if the stories are fresh or old—they only need to provide interesting conversation.

Helen argued again when I tried to convince her of the need to work at learning to narrate: "I don't see why I should have to work at this as if it were an examination in physics. I thought socializing was supposed to be fun!"

"And I suppose you want your skills at small talk to come naturally—" I replied—"as if they were encoded in your genes?"

"Well, yes. I don't want to be putting on a show I've rehearsed in advance when I'm trying to be myself. It's dishonest!"

Helen finally agreed it is sensible to work at acquiring any new skill, and that no behavior becomes second nature without practice. She went home and wrote out three stories she could conceivably tell in most social settings. She was to memorize her stories, practice telling them in front of a mirror, and tell them to me at our next session just as if we were participating together in a social conversation.

Helen's stories, like most things she did, were quite adequate. All of them were based on personal experiences.

I made her tell me her stories several times because she was tense and uncomfortable doing the unfamiliar. Finally, Helen was able to relax and feel quite comfortable as she rehearsed her material.

Helen's next assignment was to tell someone else her stories.

"That ought to work out pretty well," she said, showing a bit of tentative enthusiasm. "I'm going to an open house tonight, and I don't know most of the other guests. I'll try my stories on some of them."

Helen came to her next session beaming. For once she had felt good about a social occasion in which she was forced to talk to strangers. She reported enthusiastically that others listened to her stories, chimed in with their own, and gave every evidence of enjoying chatting with her. She had felt included in a social gathering of which she had previously known only three of the eighteen people present.

Perhaps you are having difficulty imagining how all this worked. You're thinking, What about the fact that Helen's stories were all prepared in advance? How could she be sure they would fit in? What if her stories were about—say, animals, and the others were talking about something else—baseball, or kamikaze pilots, for instance?

I had worked on this point with Helen before the party. In small talk, unlike some other forms of conversation we have studied, it is perfectly all right to tie your story loosely to the flow of things and proceed with it. This sort of talk is often desultory anyway. It frequently rambles along from subject to subject with no more to tie topics together than loose associations.

To introduce the experience you want to recount, simply say, "That reminds me of something I saw today over at the shopping center. . ." or, "For some reason, what you just described makes me think of what my doctor told me yesterday. . ." That's all the introduction you need to launch into your story.

If you bear in mind that, in small talk, you have a right to change the subject if you feel like it, you will solve the problem posed by shy, introverted people: "I can't think of anything to say on the subject others are discussing."

How do I answer that objection? "Well, then, change the subject. Nobody will mind."

Please note that such license to change the subject applies only to small talk. In other kinds of talk, you must follow more rigid rules.

Here are some stories Helen wrote out, memorized and later used satisfactorily at a party. They are reproduced approximately the way Helen told them to the group.

#1

"Al, what you said about the crime wave reminds me of my parents' effort to protect their home. When they moved to their place in the country, my dad said, 'We should get some dogs. This house is quite a distance from the watchful eye of our nearest neighbor.' So we got a pair of German Shepherd puppies. At two years old, they looked big and fierce enough to scare off any intruder.

"Well, the other day I was at my folks' house alone. I had been in the backyard, came into the house, and thought for sure I heard someone at the front door. I went and looked, and sure enough, a delivery man had the door ajar and was putting parcels inside into the hall.

"And the dogs? What were they doing? Our two fierce-looking watchdogs were on the scene all right, wagging their tails and licking the man's hands as if he were a relative. Such watchdogs!"

#2

"Tom, your earthquake experience makes me think of the day last spring when my friend and I were watching a fascinating movie in the shopping center theater. Suddenly, the projector shut off, the lights went on, and the manager stepped forward. 'Please leave the theater,' he announced. Not another word, no explanation, just, 'Please, everyone, leave the building.'

"What was it all about? A fire? We joined an orderly line and stepped out into the parking lot.

"The sky was dark brownish yellow. The crowd was excited. People were pointing to the western sky where a huge, black funnel cloud was racing toward the spot on which we stood. No one had told us we were directly in the path of a tornado! And no one had directed us to shelter. We made for a roadway with a ditch alongside. My friend had taken her shoes off in the theater and was having trouble getting them on again.

" 'Come on, Jo!' I shouted, 'hurry up and get those shoes on. We have to run. It's worth a little effort to hurry.' But the tornado was bearing down on us so we changed our course and headed for the shopping center.

" 'Maybe we can find shelter inside,' she said. Still the storm seemed determined to follow us.

"Finally I pointed my finger straight at the racing funnel and yelled, 'I command you, in Jesus' name, turn away!' I thought to myself, *You sound quite presumptuous!* Nevertheless, for whatever reason, the monster changed directions, veered off to the north, and the entire shopping center was left untouched by the storm!"

#3

"Speaking of babies, I'd like to tell you about an experience I had in the woods the other day. I was going for a walk, and I came upon a quiet little pond, nestled among the trees.

"*Keep hidden,* I thought to myself, *maybe there will be geese or ducks on the surface of that clear, lovely water.*

"I approached stealthily, keeping my feet off branches and twigs. Soon I spotted a female mallard with a brood of newly hatched ducklings swimming after her. She was alert for danger and soon became aware of my presence. Softly and swiftly she gave her babies a command, and instantly they turned their little heads down and their tails up and disappeared beneath the water, little rippling circles marking their dives.

"Almost as quickly, the mother took to the air. She made no effort to hide herself. On the contrary, she quacked loudly and flapped noisily, circling around me until she was sure I saw her. Then she flew in circles ever farther from the spot where her little ones had disappeared.

"*What a woman!* I mused. *She's offering herself and her life for her babies.* You know, she could teach something to the rest of us about unselfishness. What a contrast between the self-giving love of this mother duck and the selfish uncaring of some human mothers who sacrifice their unborn babies' lives for their own convenience!"

Self-revelation—the name of the game. Because you are a child of God, and because His very nature leads Him to reveal himself, you as a Christian must also practice openness. The things you say and do may either hide or reveal who you really are. Developing closer relationships involves revealing more and more of yourself to other people. A truly close relationship is one in which both persons practice total truthfulness. Even in small talk, you must reveal small doses of yourself to give others something to relate to.

Helen's stories are not perfect models of brilliant, sparkling small talk. However, these stories exemplify some of the functions of small talk. They are therefore included so you can learn from them.

Notice in each of these stories how Helen has revealed small bits of her inner self. Below is a list of some of the things a total stranger could learn about Helen by hearing her stories:

1. Helen's parents live nearby in the country. She probably doesn't live with them.

2. She attends the theater with her girlfriend. Helen is likely not married.
3. Helen used the name of Jesus seriously. She must be a Christian.
4. One of the issues Helen seems to care passionately about is the sacredness of human life. Moral issues seem important to her.
5. Helen enjoys walking in the woods and attending good movies.

All of that from three simple little stories!

HUMOR

The examples we have given from Helen's small talk include no jokes. Nonetheless, jokes have a place in small talk, although many Christians shy away from telling them for several reasons: First, jokes are often told at someone's expense. If your speech embarrasses or hurts another person just to gain a few moments in the social limelight, the price is too high. If the story you want to tell makes fun of some racial or cultural subgroup, make certain you don't rub a raw nerve or massage salt into an open wound. People who are battling feelings of religious, cultural, or racial inferiority in themselves, and genuine prejudice in others, are not likely to find as much humor in such stories as those of an "established" cultural group. You can usually get away with making fun of Norwegians among Norwegians. But be careful of jokes told at the expense of blacks, hispanics, or Indians. They have suffered true discrimination, and can justifiably be hurt by degrading remarks.

Second, much humor these days is immoral. I need not dwell at length on the fact that, among Christians, filthy, off-color stories have no place.

Finally, many ordinary, garden variety jokes used as small talk leave little room for self-revelation. When you tell a story you heard or read, you are telling very little about who and how you yourself are.

Humor, however, can ripple through stories of your own experiences. You do not need a punch line to get people smiling.

Notice again Helen's story of the two dogs. Her audience smiled as she pictured two huge canine oafs, acquired for their reputation as fierce watchdogs, fawning over the stranger who had calmly opened the front door and set packages inside. Such humor in personal experiences can serve as a vehicle to give others bits of information about the inner you. Such stories are a valid example of "telling each other the truth"—the truth about yourself.

PRACTICING

Satisfied with your own social talk? Or do you want to improve your skills? If you desire to change your small talk habits, to acquire the ability to ask interesting questions and to tell stories when you are socializing, you will have to work at change. As with other skills taught in this book, little will be gained by merely reading what I have written. By contrast, much can be done through practicing what you have read.

Helen practiced her small talk skills assiduously. As a result, she found her fear of group gatherings markedly reduced. In fact, at times she sought out get-togethers and found a good deal of satisfaction in just chatting with people she didn't know very well.

The most valuable result for Helen was an increase in friendships. This is not a chapter on the subject of making friends, but I can tell you briefly what Helen did. She found opportunities to talk at greater length with some of those who small talked with her. She discovered that her interests and values were shared by a few of them. Likewise, others discovered much in Helen to like and seek out. They exchanged phone numbers. Helen had lunch and coffee with people she wanted to know better. She made a point of initiating additional contacts—something she had feared doing because someone might reject her. In a very short time, Helen had developed a number of meaningful friendships, some of which were progressing toward closeness.

If you decide you want to practice small talk skills, remember to tell yourself the truth that small talk is *not* a trivial waste of time. Rather, it is a necessary social activity which gives people a chance to know each other gradually and without great threat.

Practice devising interesting questions and use them. Practice telling stories from your experiences and use them. You might feel a bit forced when you first try new social behavior. That feeling will occur often as you apply the teachings you find in this book. But as you continue to practice, what at first felt stiff and abnormal will eventually feel as much a part of you as the habits you have developed up to this point.

Practice devising questions. Write out a list of ordinary questions you might hear wherever two people who don't know each other very well are chatting. Here are some examples:

1. What do you think of the weather we've been having lately? Hot enough (or cold enough or wet enough or dry enough) for you?
2. Where do you live?
3. Were you born here?
4. Do you have a family?
5. Did you have a nice vacation?

These questions, asked over and over in everyday social contexts, are not likely to evoke much interest. So see if you can rework them or invent others which might provoke a bit more thought in the respondent. Here are some examples to get you started:

1. Do you think weather affects people's moods and personalities? What do you think the weather we've been having might do to most people's moods? [Weather is the old standby. People *are* interested in it. Might as well make it interesting.]
2. If you had your choice of any area of the country [city, state, world—if you like], where would you choose to live?
3. Do you think any special traits are particularly characteristic of people who were born here? How about yourself? Do you have these traits? Why or why not?
4. In your opinion, what is the ideal size for a family? Why do you think so? Is your family that size?
5. I understand you went to France for your vacation. Tell me,

what would you recommend I should under no circumstances miss if I would visit France?

Now you work out some additional revamping of common small talk questions. Memorize them carefully before the next occasion comes to strike up a conversation. Then go for it. Give your questions, or some of them, a try. You will very likely not have to use more than one or two. The conversation will likely take care of itself after one or two of your deftly crafted openers.

Practice telling stories. Chances are, you will find it easier to ask questions than to devise and tell good stories. That is why I recommend you give storytelling much more practice than questioning. Seek out opportunities and settings where you can tell your stories. Do as Helen did: Write out your stories at first. Unless you are already a skilled storyteller you will find it much easier to work out interesting stories from a written draft which you revise until you are satisfied.

Then memorize your stories.

I know, you'd like it all to be spontaneous. And if you are one of those fortunate folks already skilled at narrative, you can skip this hard work. But just wishing it would all come naturally doesn't make it so. That is why you should, at first, write out and memorize narratives.

Then get out and use what you have created. Remember, in the usual small talk setting, you don't need much of an excuse to change the subject. Not much more is necessary than to say, "Speaking of . . ." or "That reminds me of the time . . ." Your story will remind someone else of one and the conversation will follow on your new track for a while.

Don't fail to include small and tasteful truths about your inner self in your small talk. Reveal yourself to others. Give them something to like. There is nothing wrong with letting others know that you like to ski, that you never miss prayer meetings, or that you love good books.

Do you wish the old radio shows would come back? Are you looking for someone to go fishing with? Do you develop, enlarge, and print your own photographs? Tell people. Do winter days make you sad? Are you feeling considerable loss since your last child went off to college? Do your angel food cakes fall when you try to make them from scratch? Open up. Let people know you.

Most people don't need a caution here, but some do: Don't reveal too much of yourself too soon. There are many things appropriately reserved for relationships which have been tested a bit. Usually, good judgment will tell you what they are. Pray for guidance in the matter of what to reveal to whom and when.

FOR REVIEW, PRAYER AND DISCUSSION

1. For what kinds of people is small talk apt to present difficulties?
2. What is the difference between the difficulties of the shy and introverted and those of the type A personality, insofar as small talk is concerned?
3. What are the reasons for learning small talk?
4. Is small talk purposeless? Give reasons for your answer— i.e., give the purposes of small talk.
5. What sort of important information is small talk meant to convey to others?
6. What is a close relationship?
7. How many very close relationships do you have? If you have none or few, you are not the only one. If you have none or a few, would you like to have more? Why do you answer as you do?
8. What two skills can you develop to improve your small talk?
9. Tell how you can go about developing each one.